New Day
New Church

Ben Johnson

Book design by Melissa Mahoney

ISBN 1-885121-15-6

CTS Press
P.O. Box 520
Decatur, GA 30031

To my friend and colleague
Walter Brueggemann

TABLE OF CONTENTS

PREFACE

Most of us in mainline congregations recognize that today's generation stands at a very different place from those gone by — particularly when it comes to the work of evangelism and church growth. The world has changed. Yet, simply acknowledging these changes and the ineffectiveness of old methods does little to solve the rather pressing problems facing our ministry. I believe we must reassess our context for ministry and intentionally employ a different strategy in order to be a healthy, ministering body.

New Day, New Church represents my effort to analyze our new context for ministry, propose new initiatives, and offer practical guidance for implementing these proposals. In line with this purpose, I have divided the book into three sections: Context, Proposal, and Praxis. In the Context section I have begun with the current plight of mainline congregations and the haunting memory of the first century church, following with a description of the modern context and the kinds of persons we are trying to reach with the gospel. A companion volume, *95 Theses for the Church*, explicates many of these ideas and will, I believe, prove to be a helpful resource.

In the second section I have made a modest proposal that fits the congregations with which I am most familiar. These congregations need to recover a sense of the presence of God, develop mature disciples, shift from maintenance to mission, revitalize worship, and liberate laity for ministry in the church and in the world. These initiatives will, I believe, put us on the way to recovering the dynamic life of the early church.

In the third section I have described ways to implement each proposal, including experiences of several cutting-edge mainline congregations. These are simple, clearly outlined procedures to bring about the kind of setting in which the Spirit of God seems to work best.

I believe there are at least three ways to maximize the benefit of this book: 1) Use it as a source for an officers' retreat; 2) Distribute copies to the congregation as background for a series of sermons on Future Church; and, 3) Use the Proposal and Praxis sections for developing new initiatives in your church's ministry. This text offers three things: understanding of the context, a direction for the future, and strategies for moving into the future. A particular congregation may have a deeper interest in one of these sections than another. Begin where your sense of urgency lies.

Finally, I appreciate the help I have been given in writing this book. First, thanks to Nan, my wife, who typed the original drafts. Also, I am grateful for six students who met with me weekly to discuss the original manuscript: Zoe Anne Henderson, Paul Lang, Andras Lovas, Jeff Reynolds, Walt Tennyson, and Nancy Graham. Greg Lund assisted me with notations and quotes. Nancy Graham not only discussed the early manuscript, she has given invaluable assistance in editing this text. Many of my colleagues at Columbia Theological Seminary clarified my ideas: Walter Brueggemann, Stan Saunders, Catherine Gonzalez, Lucy Rose, Jeanne Stevenson-Moessner, Carlos Cardoza-Orlandi, George Telford, Will E. Coleman, James Hudnut-Beumler, Ben Kline, and Ron Cram. None of them, however, can be held responsible for this final version of the text. My thanks also go to the Board of Trustees at Columbia Seminary for a semester-long sabbatical to finalize this text.

BEN JOHNSON

PART I : THE CONTEXT

CHAPTER 1

A Haunting Memory for the Modern Church

In January 1991 my wife Nan and I led a small group of students into the streets, seminaries, barrios, and political havens of Central America, pursuing what Columbia Theological Seminary calls an "Alternative Context for Ministry." We traveled there for three weeks as *learners*, walking alongside natives and mission co-workers to lay hold of the multi-faceted culture and its many implications for faith.

One of our more striking experiences occurred in Nicaragua, newly emerging from civil warfare. Though the ravages of war were still evident, I found myself more perplexed by the long-term effects of a different kind of devastation: an earthquake that sent the capital of Managua reeling in 1972 and had left the nation in aftershock for 19 years.

This beautiful, largely modern city has been "re-built" since that disaster left 10,000 persons dead — but *much* has not been restored. Nowhere was this more evident than on Roosevelt Boulevard, once the pulse-racing, people-moving "Wall Street" of Nicaragua. Nineteen years after the earthquake, the imposing structures of Roosevelt Boulevard hovered over deserted avenues. Structurally unsound high-rise buildings, crumbling after upheaval and two decades without care, were plastered with government warnings to keep out.

Yet in the dust of these decaying buildings and within sight of these government warnings, families settled — laundry extended on lines across courtyards and children playing among the rubble. Because the government exerted no effort to reclaim or reconstruct these buildings, people desperate for shelter crowded into these shells of former edifices. Aware that these structures might collapse suddenly and kill them all — tonight or tomorrow or the next day — men, women, and children continued to eat and sleep there at their own peril.

In recent months as I have reflected on the future of the church, the images of Roosevelt Boulevard have sprung to my remembrance. Like Managua, contemporary Western culture has weathered a devastating shake-up. And the Christian church, once its pulse-racing, people-moving center, now stands as a shell of its former glory. Though prophets and scholars post warnings that such a harshly shaken structure cannot "bear up" forever, many contemporary Christians continue to function within this shell of the church and its denominations at their own peril. Indeed, if we do not intentionally reclaim and reconstruct the contemporary church in the power of the Holy Spirit, its crumbling structure may well collapse, crushing many innocent people with it.

Yet how do we "reclaim" and "reconstruct"? As we grope in these days of uncertainty, I am drawn to the New Testament portrait of God's relentless, unleashed power. Here we find hope to release us from the caved-in cathedrals of "former things." Here, from the platform of Pentecost (Acts 2), the rooftop visions of Joppa (Acts 10), and the council floors of Jerusalem (Acts 15), we unlock the secret power which can restore us.

Truly, there is something haunting about the memory of the church's birth, its communal life, original vision, and spectacular accomplishments. No matter how we view the Acts narrative, where this story unfolds, we cannot help being deeply impressed with the Christian community's confidence in its risen Lord, the clarity with which it perceived its mission, and the zeal with which members engaged in their calling. The Acts narrative paints the picture of a community embodying Christ and functioning as his body in the world.

In sharp contrast to the vitality and vision of the early

church stand numerous struggling, mainline congregations at the threshold of the twenty-first century — dwelling in the decay of former things. To sharpen this comparison of today's church with that of the first century, I invite you to reflect on the truths expressed in a fictional account of the "Bankruptcy of the United Church of Christ."

In a half-serious, half-humorous manner, the Rev. Robert G. Kempler wrote the forward-looking 1992 article, "A History of the United Church of Christ 1957-2007."[1] This imaginative piece covers the period from the denomination's most recent merger to 15 years beyond the original critique.

The writer cited a central event in this 50-year history as "The Ruin," the monetary bankruptcy of the denomination. In 1994, Kempler speculated, the UCC filed bankruptcy, realizing that even withdrawing cash from the Pension Fund could not ward off its dissolution. By the end of the year the entire denomination was dismantled — no agencies, publications, conferences, or offices.

Looking backward from 2007 a few things became obvious, Kempler noted:

☀ Everyone had blamed everyone else: the pro-New York group blamed the pro-Cleveland crowd, bureaucrats blamed local churches, Biblicists blamed the apostasy of the denomination, and the list of culprits goes on.

☀ Program units had demanded more and more autonomy. Issues in one decade were institutionalized by the next: race, economics, justice, women's issues, sexual orientation. What was "in" became "fixed."

☀ Special interests had taken control. The UCC became an amalgam of sects each demanding that the church be formed to support this special concern.

In summary, The Ruin came upon the UCC because of a series of "neglects" — its history, principles, heritage. The writer suggested to fellow strugglers that they had neglected the things they held in common. The warring groups divided the Christian faith in racial, ethnic, gender, liberal, and conservative slices.

Looking back from 2007, insiders recalled that in 1994 a few persons thought they would soon get back to business as usual, but such was not to be. "What was called for was a new denomination for a new day. We were beyond the point of patching and pasting."

Among the needs for such a new day were: 1) Leadership, 2) Structural changes, 3) Financial Reforms, 4) Assemblies, 5) Outreach, and 6) Faith. In short, a few visionaries saw that what happened in the years from 1994-2007 was not the dismantling of the UCC; instead *The Ruin precipitated a restoration* because followers began to look anew at the basics of the faith and the convictions they held in common.

This imaginative apocalypse for the UCC points to the enormous challenges that lie before most mainline churches. Pieces of this story readily align with the history of most established churches in the United States. This story of The Ruin challenges all of us to rethink how we "do church." First, the shock of The Ruin challenges the church to examine its life. The glitches in our life together will become obvious. We must, I believe, return to the *basics* of being church to discover in our day what it means to be the people of God.

Second, the church must face the reality that ministry today occurs in a very different context from any other time in the American experience. The church exists in a post-Christian, "post-Constantinian," secular context.

Third, in order to reach secular persons outside the door of the church, the typical congregation must face changes in its ethos, worship style, forms of ministry, and in the way it views the secular community. Without these changes in our church paradigm our congregations will continue to experience decline and possibly The Ruin!

Even though these proposals create feelings of anxiety and resistance, we must change. The future depends

NEW DAY - NEW CHURCH

upon it. The old ways no longer work and new ways must be born out of the agony of change precipitated by the gospel.

A RETURN TO BASICS

If the crisis of the church today calls us to return to basics, nothing will help our vision more than a review of the life and ministry of the Acts church. Pentecost marks the birth of the church just as Christmas denotes the birth of the Savior. The Spirit came upon the womb of the virgin to conceive and give birth to the Son, and the same Spirit came upon the community of disciples to conceive and give birth to the Body of Christ, the church. This corporate body was infused with the Spirit of God as was Jesus at his baptism; its task was to continue the ministry begun by Jesus of Nazareth. The mission that began at one moment in history continues in history through the Body of Christ.

This vision of the incarnation led Dietrich Bonhoeffer to describe the church as "Christ existing as community," that is, a corporate body of believers alive to his presence and responsive to his guidance.[2] Karl Barth emphasized the same vision when he spoke of the church as "his earthly form of existence." Through the action of the Spirit, God has created another body, a corporate body, in which Christ continues to live and through which he continues his mission. With this perception of the church we begin our examination of the character and actions of this community. What was this early church like?

FILLED WITH DIVINE PRESENCE

The first century church was filled with the sense of the divine, an awareness born of the Spirit: "When the day of Pentecost had come, they were all together in one place. . . All of them were filled with the Holy Spirit and began to speak in other languages, as the Spirit gave them ability" (Acts 2:1,4). The Holy Spirit gave them an awareness of the immediate presence of the risen and living Jesus Christ. He was as real to them in the Spirit as he had been in the flesh.

Jesus of Nazareth, the Christ, who had come in the flesh came again in the Spirit to continue the work he had begun. Is there any wonder that the early church closely identified the Holy Spirit with the risen Christ? Jesus had promised, "I will not leave you orphaned; I am coming to you" (John 14:18). Jesus had said, "...I am with you always, to the end of the age" (Matt. 28:20).

Several non-negotiable convictions gripped this body of believers. The Holy Spirit was indeed the Spirit of Christ. He had come to take up his abode in them. The Spirit would guide them and empower them as Jesus always had. And, finally, they understood the Spirit to be completing in their community the work that Jesus of Nazareth had begun in his flesh. As David Bosch notes about the early church, "The Spirit not only initiates mission, he also guides the missionaries about where they should go and how they should proceed. The missionaries are not to execute their own plans but have to wait on the Spirit to direct them."[3]

Along with the completion of the work of Christ, members of the early church also experienced the Spirit as a new center of authority and power. Dutch theologian Hendrikus Berkhoff says,

> "The Spirit is far more than an instrumental entity, the subjective reverse of Christ's work. His coming to us is a great new event in the series of God's saving acts. He creates a world of his own, a world of conversion, experience, sanctification; of tongues, prophesy, and miracles; of mission; of upbuilding and guiding the church, etc. He appoints ministers; he organizes; he illumines, inspires, and sustains; he intercedes for the saints

and helps them in their weaknesses; he searches everything, even the depths of God; he guides into all truths; he grants a variety of gifts; he convinces the world; he declares the things that are to come. In short, as the Johannine Jesus says: He who believes in me will also do the works that I do; and greater works than these will he do, because I go to the Father' (John 14:12).[4]

This summary of the activity of the Spirit summarizes the consciousness of the early church. In all these ways they experienced the presence in their midst carrying out the mission of Jesus Christ. This evidence gave them courage to believe that Jesus was alive in their community and also in each of them as members of the community.

What has happened to this consciousness of the presence of Jesus in our midst? Consider the questions that will begin to uncover an awareness of his presence:

1. Do the members of our church exhibit an awareness of Christ? Do they speak of him as a present reality?

2. Are we aware of the presence of the living Christ among us in worship?

3. In planning the ministry of the church, do we ask for and expect Christ to show us what to do?

4. What would happen in our congregation if members began to live in the consciousness of Christ?

THE CHURCH PRAYED

Prayer was the church's initial response to its awareness of the divine presence! Because the first century church lived in the awareness of the risen Christ, it was diligent in prayer. Prayer for this community meant communication with the present but unseen Lord. Confident of their participation in his mission to the world, believers spoke with him as naturally as when he was with them in the flesh. "They discovered very early that only prayer was both personal enough to get them unself-centered and comprehensive enough to include all aspects of the fallen world in the personal/political action of Messiah," explains Eugene Peterson.[5] This natural communication with Christ appears continuously in their life together.

For example, this community was born in prayer. "All these (disciples of Jesus) were constantly devoting themselves to prayer" (Acts 1:14). The disciples, after the ascension of Jesus, went to the Upper Room in obedience to his command and persisted in prayer.

Prayer nurtured this church. When new believers were baptized, they entered a community of prayer and fellowship and found support and hope. According to the Acts account, those who were baptized devoted themselves "to the apostles' teaching and fellowship, to the breaking of bread and the prayers" (Acts 2:42).

The early church prayed when members were persecuted (Acts 4:23-31). When the Jewish authorities sought to erase the small body of believers, the whole church brought to God their pain. The dimension of the Holy was accessible through prayer; the Transcendent was near as they expressed themselves in praise!

Prayer gave birth to the missionary movement of the church. At Antioch in Syria a small band of disciples fasted, prayed, and awaited guidance for its mission (Acts 13:1-3). "It [was] the Spirit who embolden[ed] previously timid disciples."[6] In the midst of their worship the Spirit spoke. In obedience to the Spirit's direction the disciples sent forth Barnabas and Saul with prayer and the laying on of hands. In the unfolding story of the church, there seems to be a rhythm — crisis, prayer, renewal, mission. Does this rhythm speak to us today?

Answering these questions may be revealing about the role of prayer in the church today:

1. What is the role of prayer in our congregation?

2. To what degree does our congregation depend upon prayer for guidance in our ministry?

3. How important is prayer in the life of members?

4. What differences can we imagine if the ministries of our congregation were saturated with prayer?

WITNESSES TO THE LIVING CHRIST

The apostolic congregation witnessed to the reality of Jesus Christ. From the beginning Peter set the example for the church when he spoke to the crowd on the day of Pentecost. "...[L]isten to what I have to say: Jesus of Nazareth, a man attested to you by God with deeds of power, wonders, and signs that God did through him among you, as you yourselves know...This Jesus God raised up, and of that all of us are witnesses" (Acts 2:22, 32). Because their life was centered in the divine presence, they could not suppress their witness. The Spirit always compels the church to witness. They spoke freely and naturally of one whom they knew and one in whom their life was centered. So urgent was the witness that they spoke to the devout, to the semi-religious, and to pagans alike.

At Pentecost, Peter bore witness to the devout Jews who had come to the festival from every nation under heaven. He grounded his testimony in the scriptures: "This is what was spoken through the prophet Joel " (Acts 2:16-21).

Imagine the courage it took for Peter to stand before this group of culturally diverse persons and tell the story of Jesus. Never before had he preached Christ; nor had he given testimony to his death and resurrection; he had no idea what would happen; there was no precedent for how the Holy Spirit would work through the gospel. Yet one thing he knew: the one who had been caught and executed was now risen and reigning, and in his power Peter spoke.

Since this preacher could not predict how his hearers would be affected by the story of Jesus' life, death, and resurrection, how amazed he must have been when three thousand persons responded to the life-changing message!

After the explosion of faith ignited by Peter's witness, fear, jealousy, and hostility erupted in the Jewish community. They persecuted the young church and under the persecution all the believers left Jerusalem except the apostles. But as they traveled through the countryside they gave witness to their faith. "Those who were scattered...proclaim[ed] the word" (Acts 8:4).

The followers of Christ witnessed to the pagans as evidenced by Paul's address to the Athenians (17:16-31). He proclaimed the gospel to Greek philosophers and poets and invited them to believe in Jesus and the resurrection. This church also witnessed to Jews, Samaritans, and Greek sympathizers. These Christians faced the same question we face in today's secular age: "How do we effectively communicate the message of reconciliation and life to the secular unchurched people who have no Christian background, memory, or vocabulary, the millions of 'ignostics' who do not know what we are talking about?"[7] To all who would listen, they told the story of Jesus' life, death, and resurrection and many who heard their witness became believers. Their witness was urgent, confident, persistent, and effective.

To bridge the gap between the early church and our church today, we might ask ourselves these questions:

1. How does our church give witness to the living Christ?

2. How could all the members of our church give a more effective witness to the risen Christ?

3. How are members of our church encouraged to witness?

4. Would a different structure within our church strengthen our ability to witness to Christ?

DEMONSTRATION OF COMPASSION

The first century church not only gave verbal witness to Christ but it fleshed out the gospel by deeds of compassion. For a church to be effective, it must both speak the message and demonstrate it. Unlike today's church, the first century church had no ongoing struggle between camps for those who emphasized proclaiming the gospel and those who emphasized enacting the gospel through compassion and activism. Lesslie Newbigin wrote, "If I am not mistaken, the conflict between these two ways of understanding mission is profoundly weakening the Church's witness."[8]

Two instances of compassion in the early days of the church claim our attention: healing a lame man and caring for widows. The lame man lay outside the door of the temple. Daily he was seen by those who entered the temple for prayer. For years he had been helpless, hopeless, and reduced to begging. He represents all the marginalized persons in society.

At three o'clock one afternoon Peter and John went to the temple for prayer. As they entered, the man motioned to them for an offering. Peter stopped, looked at him, and spoke: "I have no silver or gold, but what I have I give you; in the name of Jesus Christ of Nazareth, stand up and walk" (Acts 3:6). In this encounter, Peter fleshed out the Spirit of Christ who always reached out to the poor, the marginalized, and the broken in society.

The church's response to the widows reveals another kind of compassion. The Greek widows complained that they were being neglected in the distribution of food. In response to this genuine need and potential conflict, the early church set aside deacons to care for those neglected women. They were appointed to make sure that all the widows received a fair distribution of food. By showing justice and compassion the church made visible and tangible the presence of the living Christ. The practice of caring for the poor in the early Christian communities was unique in that society, notes Martin Hengel.[9] This church experienced continuity between the presence of God, prayer, witness, and deeds of compassion.

In fact, expressions of compassion gave validity to their verbal witness. The faithful re-presentation of Jesus silenced the accusation of hypocrisy and positively encouraged faith in Christ.

Examine the ways in which your congregation shows the love of God to persons in need.

1. To whom do we minister in the name of Christ?

2. How does our church demonstrate the Spirit of Jesus Christ to the poor or marginalized?

3. Do members of our congregation give evidence of sacrificial service for Christ?

4. How can we more faithfully re-present Christ in our community?

INTEGRITY

The first century church guarded its integrity in order to protect its witness. They exercised discipline in an effort to keep the witness pure. Perhaps no issue creates more pain for us today than the discipline of members. Relativism and pluralism have unnerved us with respect to making judgments about fellow members of the church. "In a pluralist society, any confident affirmation of the truth is met by the response, 'Why should I believe this rather than that?'"[10] As a consequence, almost any behavior has become acceptable. Discipline proves essential if the church is to maintain its integrity.

In the early days of the church, two members sold a piece of land and claimed to bring the whole price to the church. Secretly, they had kept back part of the money for themselves. When questioned about the transaction they lied. Quick judgment came upon them. Both died (Acts 5:1-11). As a consequence, respect and awe filled all the other members.

The issue of integrity reaches beyond the offering of gifts to support the mission. Paul believed that a healthy congregation validated the gospel, thus his emphasis on integrity in congregational life. Likewise, a disobedient congregation betrayed the gospel and called into question the witness of every Christian. (The letters to the church at Corinth illustrate this concern.) A church without integrity cannot give a transformative witness to the world!

Consider these difficult questions as they affect our congregations today:

1. What examples of congregational betrayal can you identify?

2. What effect does the failure of a Christian or a church have on our witness to the gospel?

3. How should offenders be disciplined?

TOTAL INVOLVEMENT

The first century church involved all of its members in ministry. "Now there are varieties of gifts, but the same Spirit; and there are varieties of services, but the same Lord; and there are varieties of activities, but it is the same God who activates all of them in everyone...All these are activated by one and the same Spirit, who allots to each one individually just as the Spirit chooses" (1 Cor. 12:4-6, 11). Each had a gift, a place, and a role in witnessing for Christ.

The ministry of Philip illustrates the distribution of the ministry throughout the Body of Christ. Because he was a man filled with faith and the Holy Spirit, the apostles chose him to be a deacon. He willingly served the widows until the persecution. When the persecution came, all believers fled Jerusalem, except the apostles. Philip went into Samaria. He gave such a convincing testimony to Christ that numerous Samaritans believed (Acts 8:9-24). After they were established in the faith, the Spirit in a strange manner sent Philip away into the desert toward Gaza. There he spoke with an Ethiopian eunuch, a man of great power and prestige in the court of Queen Candace (Acts 8:26-40). The eunuch believed in Christ and requested baptism. In these two instances Philip, a lay person, illustrates how the early Christians joined social ministry with evangelistic witness through the power of Christ.

The church that emerged in later centuries all too often encouraged a passive laity. The common vision of church members extended no further than attending worship, giving money, and living as good citizens. This misunderstanding of mission and lay involvement reduced ministry to the role of professionally trained clergy. If ministry remains the sole responsibility of professionals, the mission of Christ will be doomed to failure.

Consider your congregation with respect to lay involvement:

1. Do members of our church have a sense of being called by God for ministry in the world?

2. What evidence of ministry in daily life do we see in our congregation? How can a more intentional ministry be emphasized?

3. What changes would it make in our church if all the members were involved in the mission of Christ?

LED BY THE SPIRIT

This early community of Christ lived with the conviction that he directed the mission with his presence in their midst. Evidence of the Spirit's guidance permeates the stories remembered and told by the early church.

We have noted Philip's experience in Samaria when the Spirit led him to the desert to witness to the eunuch (Acts 8:26ff). The Spirit's direction surrounded Peter's visit to the house of Cornelius. God directed Cornelius to send messengers to bring Peter to his home. While the

messengers were en route, Peter had a vision that prepared him for their invitation. During Peter's sermon in
Cornelius's house, the Spirit fell upon the listeners giving
them joy and ecstatic utterances (Acts 10:1-48).
Occurrences like these confirmed the church's belief that
the Spirit of the risen Christ guided believers in their mission and went with them wherever they went.

In addition to the guidance of the Spirit in the
Cornelius episode, we later discover that the missionary
movement of the Christian church began when the Spirit
led a small group of disciples in Antioch in Syria to com-
mission Saul and Barnabas as missionaries (Acts 13:1-4).

A further evidence of the church's conviction of divine
intervention in their work deserves mention. On the second missionary journey, Paul and his companion passed
through Phrygia and Galatia because they "had been for-
bidden by the Holy Spirit to speak the word in Asia" (Acts
16:6). Although the Spirit refused permission to witness
in one place, he directed them to another. Perhaps the
early church had such astounding success because they
looked to Christ for guidance in the fulfillment of the ministry.

In what ways do we discern the presence of the Spirit
in our ministry choices?

1. Do we have a sense of guidance in our mission to
the community? To the world?

2. How do we discern what the risen Christ is saying
to us today?

3. How can we begin to focus our ministry in response
to the guidance of Jesus Christ?

CHANGED LIVES

The early church demonstrated the Holy Spirit's phenomenal power to change persons' lives. They understood
their mission was to make disciples of Jesus Christ. In
numerous ways they addressed this task — preaching,

teaching, healing, feeding the poor. In all these ministries the community had one clear goal in mind — to make disciples of Christ. Whether through the preaching of Peter at Pentecost or the witness of Philip in the desert or through the missionary journeys of Paul, they called forth new believers whose lives were remade.

The faith and sacrifice of every new believer nurtured the vision and the enthusiasm of the original followers. Christ indeed continued his ministry through them. Could they have sustained their vision if they never saw new persons initiated into the faith?

These tangible demonstrations of Christ's presence not only encouraged faith but created expectancy. Whether they gave witness, engaged in worship, or distributed food, they expected persons to be touched by Christ, to believe, and be changed by his power. How impoverished are churches that no longer expect the presence of Christ and never see lives transformed.

Examine your ministry of transformation:

1. What expectation does our church have that persons will be changed through our ministry?

2. How would our congregation welcome and nurture a new adult believer?

3. When is the last time our church witnessed a person truly changed by an encounter with Jesus Christ?

From First Century to Twenty-First Century

Pointing to the first century church as a model raises serious objections for many persons. Some ask, "How can a pre-modern church serve this age with its sophistication, technology, and economic resources?" The objections generally focus on distance in time, change in context, and difference in goals. The distance spans almost twenty centuries. How could a two-thousand-year-old strategy aid us today? Furthermore, argues the skeptic, the context in which they worked was so vastly different from ours; they believed in a three-story universe with heaven above, hell beneath, and the world of spirits in between; belief in miracles was commonplace for them but not for us today.

We must also acknowledge that the vitality found in the Acts church did not flow unabated. The letters of Paul provide ample evidence that his congregations faced problems and often failed in their witness. The Pastoral Epistles seem to indicate a growing spirit of order that quickly hardened into a dead form. Second and third generations of renewal movements always lack the vitality and vision of the founders. But does there ever come a time that we do not need to return to the scene of our birth, fill our minds with images of "the church in the power of the Spirit," and pray that we may receive that same Spirit and find appropriate forms for its expression today?

Perhaps these objections would carry weight if we aimed to use the New Testament picture of the church as a blueprint or make it an ideal to achieve. But we don't intend to imitate its actions, only to recover its dynamic life. The center of this congregation was Christ, the risen Christ who was spiritually present to individuals and even more profoundly present in the gathered community. The consciousness of his presence pervaded their life.

What could be more potent at the dawning of a new millennium than the recovery of a profound Christ-consciousness in the congregation? He is alive today as he was the day of his resurrection; he is present among us as he was then. The intervening years may have from time to time dulled the church's consciousness of his presence but a recovery of this Christ-awareness can still provide the church power for its mission.

This radical call does not insinuate that God's people have been unaware of Christ. Many have lived in his presence, but the corporate life of the church often proceeds with little or no consciousness of him in our midst. Yet, the recovery of the divine presence will not come from trumped up efforts to believe, but through repentance and faith and grace. A recovery of the presence will be the generous gift of a gracious God! With the presence will also come all the characteristics of life and vitality experienced in the first century community!

CHAPTER 2

A Different Church, a Different World

"Can our kind of church change our kind of world?" This question, posed by Sam Shoemaker more than six decades ago, has as much relevance today as it did then.[1] Trying to make sense of the loss of vitality and vision of the early church poses a pressing and persistent problem to mainline congregations. Even taking into account the natural evolution toward form and structure in the New Testament, the loss of focus, consciousness of presence, and effectiveness in ministry forces us to confess that something seems to be missing today.

In *The Once and Future Church*, Loren Mead presents a tempting diagnosis of the new situation in which the church ministers. He suggests that a major shift in the cultural context directly shapes the church's self-image and missional involvement.

According to Mead, the apostolic church understood itself as an *ecclesia*, a community of called-out persons. By their conversion to Jesus Christ, they were called out of the world (meaning the Greco-Roman culture) into an intimate fellowship in Christ. In this fellowship, they found support, instruction, and spiritual nurture. They understood themselves as the Body of Christ.

Their mission: to re-present Jesus Christ to the world. The place of mission was clearly defined for all the members. The mission began at the door of the church. Ministry in a pagan, pluralistic, and hostile world, daily exposed the young church to tests that threatened its very existence. Yet, when this small group of fledgling disciples departed from worship, they courageously engaged in the mission. Mission commenced with the benediction.

The subjects directed their missional activity toward

needy persons around them. As the Book of Acts clearly details, they showed the compassion of Christ to the poor, hungry, powerless, and those ignored by dominant society. By their heroic, self-sacrificing demonstration of Christ's love, they shocked the pagan world. Their lives stood in stark contrast to the selfish, barbarous lives of the pagans around them.

Living lives of moral purity, they refused to bow to Caesar even at the risk of death. The Greek word for "witness" is the source of our English word, "martyr." Christians also witnessed through devoting their lives to compassionate service. These living manifestations of Christ not only drew startled responses from the pagans but their heroic dedication provoked questions about their faith. The ensuing conversations, called "witness," further awakened and informed those in their circles of influence. The multiplication of these simple, direct witnesses to the living Christ, caused the church to grow at an amazing rate. To a large extent, the effectiveness of their witness grew out of their understanding that the mission lay immediately outside the door.

THE SHIFT

The church's successful challenge to the Empire resulted in a dramatic and perhaps disastrous shift in missionary perspective. To grasp the full impact of the change that occurred requires a brief review of the movement's history. By the early years of the fourth century, the Christian movement had made such an impressive and potent witness to Christ that the Empire was shaken. The Emperor Constantine embraced the faith and in the year 313 A.D. declared Christianity the official religion of the Empire. With this edict, the whole Roman Empire was "Christianized" overnight. Just as Christians had professed faith at the risk of their lives, now those who resisted baptism did so at the threat of their lives. Quite a shift!

What happened to the small, intimate group of devout disciples requires little imagination. Swelled by masses of ignorant, undisciplined converts who knew nothing of the living presence of Christ, the passionate fellowship of committed believers was diluted. This mass conversion, created by the Emperor's edict, not only watered down the fellowship but also eroded the sacrificial lifestyle of the early Christian disciples. The flood of pagan culture that immersed the small fellowship of devout Christians led many faithful believers to flee to the desert to escape the apostasy and to seek God in solitude and prayer. Many believed the end of history to be immediate.

According to Mead, the most disastrous consequence of this Constantinian shift was a radical change in the understanding of mission. First, the evangelistic mission could no longer be "outside the door" because by the Emperor's decree the whole Empire was declared Christian. With this declaration the whole populace understood that to be a citizen of the Empire was to be a Christian. Yet, the citizens did not know the faith nor live the life of the baptized that had marked the church's first two centuries of existence. Because of the Emperor's fiat, citizens of the Empire were no longer subjects for evangelization.

Another change occurred with this Empire-embracing edict — the members of the congregation no longer had responsibility for the mission. Monks, bishops, priests, and sometimes soldiers now took on that responsibility. The demands placed on the baptized required them to be good citizens, attend worship, and provide financial support for the mission. This perversion of discipleship reduced the laity to passive spectators.

With the Christianization of the Empire, the lay task of evangelization evaporated. In the space of a few decades, the place of mission shifted from the front door of the church to the frontier of the Empire. The role of the laity changed from being daring missionaries to being passive recipients of the sacraments and the active task of providing financial support for the mission. Responsibility for the mission shifted from the whole people of God to a select group called "clergy."

Mead contends that "our task is no less than the re-invention of the church."[2] It cannot be renewed or revived but must be remade. By this he means the re-creation of the apostolic congregation that recognizes its mission as being outside the door. Churches in the West stand once again in a missionary situation. Mead forces us to address the slow erosion of vision and vitality in the institutional church. For too long we have equated member-ship with discipleship. No longer can we delude ourselves that everyone who has been baptized is a faithful believer, knowledgeable in the faith, and involved in the mission. Neither can we rest in the heresy that responsibility for the mission resides solely in the hands of the ordained. Baptism marks the beginning of mission by joining "a fragmentary and incomplete human life with the fullness of life and the perfect glory of God."[3]

OUR INHERITANCE

Historians may argue about the accuracy of Mead's interpretation, but the Constantinian charges cannot be denied. Our churches falsely believe that those outside the door no longer require evangelization. The mission seems to have shifted to the frontier, presumably being carried on by someone else — either the pastor, the mis-sionary, or denominational leaders.

For the sake of analysis, assume that Mead has cor-rectly discovered a source of the mainline malaise. How do churches function as a consequence of this Constantinian shift? Or, to ask the question another way: what have congregations in mainline denominations inherited from this Constantinian shift?

Would it be fair to say that an institution has replaced the dynamic fellowship of believers? Have we substituted a hierarchical clergy for the participation of the whole people of God? Has the experience of the living presence of Christ given way to doctrine that no longer mediates an encounter with God? Has the church exchanged its missional fervor for a maintenance mentality? Has the church been content with verbal pronouncements as substitutes for courageous sacrifice? And have we depended upon human creativity and ingenuity rather than the Holy Spirit?

AN EXAMPLE

Churches that flee to the suburbs in hopes of finding instant success in membership growth and financial stability often discover the need for more than members and money. One minister describes his experience of ministry in such a church:

> I know something about the church. I am especially familiar with one suburban congregation with a worship attendance of 130 people, steeped in a rich history, and located in a fast growing upper-income community near Philadelphia, Pennsylvania.
>
> I know this congregation well. I have been their pastor for more than a dozen years. In 1975 the church moved from a historic setting in downtown Philadelphia, purchased 15 acres of land, and built a stunningly attractive facility.
>
> The game plan was...build it and they will come!
>
> Then, the game plan was...call a young pastor and they will come! Then, the game plan was...establish the right goals and objectives and they will come!
>
> Then, the game plan was...provide the right kind of ministries and they will come!
>
> Some came. Some did not. Some moved on. Some remained. Some came from other churches.

Some moved on to other churches. Today, our congregation remains a vital congregation. There is a healthy sense of ministry and mission among our members. Our congregation has experienced spiritual and numerical growth. The future seems promising. But the real question remains, "Can our kind of church change our kind of world?"

Three different but complementary experiences underscored the urgency and relevance of the question, "Can our kind of church change our kind of world?"

A young man began attending the church. He could only remember going to a church once or twice when he was a small boy. He had no Christian memory of Sunday School, Bible stories, or worship experiences. Immersion in contemporary culture had robbed him of the prayers, the hymns, and the language of worship. Doctrines expressed from the pulpit fell on deaf ears because he did not know the meaning of the words. As George Hunter notes, in Western culture, a "secularization of consciousness...has now prevailed for three or four generations."[4] Many congregations remain totally unprepared to minister to a person not reared in the church. Their culture and programs were aimed at the churched, not the unchurched.

A second discovery reinforced the first. After a careful search within the congregation the pastor found very few people who invited friends or neighbors to attend church with them. Most members seemed to feel that their faith was a private matter between them and God and they should not intrude into the lives of non-church members. This group within the church lacked the energy to communicate faith to others in a contagious and compelling way. Whether their inability stemmed from embarrassment or unwillingness, the pastor was uncertain. The survey seemed to indicate to the minister that the congregation was content with itself and ingrown, an island unto itself, uninterested and incapable of impacting the world around it. By contrast, the early church's identity "was not in their buildings or programs but in the way that they brought new life to others."[5]

The third experience deepened the suspicion that this church lacked the courage and conviction to challenge today's world. A group of leaders convened to discuss how the church could be faithful in its witness. From this collaboration a number of ideas emerged: build an addition to the education facility; train new leadership; establish clearly defined goals; begin new, relevant programs; improve existing projects.

As the minister reviewed the proposals, it dawned upon him that the group had not mentioned the one thing that empowers and revitalizes the church — prayer! Had this church divested itself of its primary resource? Had it forgotten its calling to discern God's will? The early church rooted itself in prayer. "What a wonderful example for Christian churches today that sit in their modern upper rooms worrying about their survival instead of praying for the power to launch out on the journey with Christ."[6]

What do these three experiences suggest to us about the state of the church, not only of the suburban church in Pennsylvania but also rural, small town, and urban congregations? How many of our congregations have either forgotten or neglected the spiritual roots that develop mature disciples? Have not most of our mainline churches concluded that faith is a private matter and should not be shared with others? And, have not most congregations specialized in ministry to the baptized and ignored those who do not know the basics of the faith? Can this kind of church make a difference in our kind of world?

'OUR KIND OF WORLD'

Renewing the church for ministry in today's world not only must take into account the inner life of the church, but effective ministry must also look honestly at the world, that is, the particular place in which the church carries out its mission. The world in which the church ministers has changed drastically and rapidly. Secularization, globalization, the communication and information explosion, the multiplication of special interest groups, and the immigration of Asians, South Americans, Muslims, and other ethnic groups into the United States have fueled contextual changes unthinkable just a few decades ago.

The context of ministry has changed and that change cannot be reversed, so we must adapt our vision and methods of outreach to a new situation. Since our social situation, our geographical setting, and our place in time so powerfully shape any evangelistic endeavor, these changes force us to revise our vision, style, and method of reaching persons with the gospel. The context of ministry in the United States has been labeled as Post-Christian, Post-Denominational Loyalty, and Pluralistic. Perhaps a brief definition of these terms will aid our discussion.

POST-CHRISTIAN

To define our era as "post-Christian" refers to the end of Christendom, a period of time that began with Constantine's embrace of the Christian religion for the entire Roman Empire. From the fourth century to the twentieth, the Christian church exercised a great deal of power and influence both socially and politically in the Western world.

For most of these sixteen centuries the Western world has understood itself in Christian categories. God was the unquestioned Creator; humans were responsible to God; history embodied the working out of a divine purpose. The West no longer understands itself to be Christian; its foundation no longer rests on belief in a

Creator who providentially works out a purpose in history.

The unquestioned moral right of the Christian church in Western society has been undermined. The Western world no longer recognizes the tenets of the Christian faith as the basis for making moral decisions and governing human relationships. The twenty-first century West has been lost to the church and to Christian categories of thought.

Two major movements have shattered the monolithic structure of medieval Christendom — the Protestant Reformation and the Enlightenment. Reformation thinkers raised serious questions about the authority of the Pope and the religious domination of the Roman church. With the help of secular princes the reformers threw off the yoke of the Roman Catholic church's domination.

The Reformation by an appeal to the authority of scripture liberated the citizenry from the domination of the Pope, but it also opened the door for other forces to erode core Christian beliefs. Once the central authority of the papacy had been undercut, the door was opened for competing interpretations of scripture and divergent lifestyles. Further erosion occurred with Enlightenment thinkers in the seventeenth and eighteenth centuries.

The Enlightenment, the other formative influence, did not set out to destroy the influence of the church. Rather, leaders of the Enlightenment sought to make a place for intellectual and cultural creativity, free from the censorship of the church. In place of the authoritative Pope or the authoritative revelation in scripture, Enlightenment thinkers substituted human reason. Truth for them was the product of reason. These movements brought to maturity what we now know as secularism, an understanding of the world based on human reason rather than the divine revelation in scripture.

With belief in God and church undermined, people began to look to subhuman life — plants, animals, and objects — to find validation for life. Our modern fascination with material things, from consumerism to ecology, are manifestations of this focus. Increasingly, "humanity derived its existence and validity from 'below' and no longer 'from above.'"[7]

We cannot say for sure when Christendom ended. Its demise may still be in progress. Whatever that status may be, there has been a cultural shift away from the church and a rejection of Christian norms for behavior and lifestyle.

What does post-Christendom mean for evangelism and the renewal of the church? First of all, it emphasizes that the church cannot depend upon the culture to assist with its task of evangelization. In public school classrooms scripture reading, prayer, and worship are strictly limited by law. Not too long ago all these practices were as common as taking the roll in homeroom. Without these practices non-churched persons have minimal exposure to Christian teaching.

In addition to these changes the church also faces the loss of privileged status in the society. "As long as the Church is content to offer its beliefs modestly as simply one of the many brands available in the ideological supermarket, no offense is taken. But the affirmation that the truth revealed in the gospel ought to govern public life is offensive."[8]

The time may be nearer than we can imagine when church property will be taxed and church members will lose tax credit for benevolent contributions. What will these developments mean for a church already struggling to meet its financial responsibilities? Will this drive the church to new forms of pastoral leadership, new places for meeting, and a rude awakening to our missionary situation?

Furthermore, the church as an institution and the clergy as designated leaders will meet with increasing hostility in the decades ahead. This hostility will likely remove the clergy privilege of non-taxable income for housing. A couple of decades ago it would have been unthinkable for clergy to be sued in a civil court for malpractice. Not only is this a present fact but it probably represents a trend. Couple with these personal issues of the clergy the efforts of special interest groups to have "In God we trust" expunged from our coins and similar efforts to remove Christian symbols from all publicly owned buildings and land.

These changes in context underscore the fact that we minister in an increasingly missionary situation. What is the difference in ministry in this setting and one in Zambia, Pakistan, or Thailand? How do we evangelize persons who do not share our fundamental convictions? These questions puzzled the suburban Philadelphia congregation when the young man who visited their worship service did not know the language, form, or substance of the service.

To evangelize in a post-Christian world, the church must find ways to communicate the gospel in its most basic form. If a culture does not expose persons to the faith and does not nurture Christian values, the church must find ways to teach the basics of the faith. "We Christians represent the ultimate reality, revealed in Jesus Christ, for whom all people search. We are called, in this generation, to mount a great movement for the re-evangelization of the West," writes George Hunter.[9] Perhaps the church should never have expected the culture to do its training for discipleship.

Second, the church that responds to the felt needs of non-church persons will give a powerful witness to the gospel. Christians have always made their strongest witness through acts of compassion and sacrifice. Providing support groups for divorcees, battered women, drug abusers, and other suffering persons will demonstrate the gospel convincingly to persons who do not know the vocabulary of faith. Support groups, staffed by believing Christians, provide both personal and psychological help as well as an exposure to the faith.

Third, in a post-Christian culture, the minister and worship committee must assume that non-church persons do not understand the language, liturgy, or sacraments of the church. To create a sense of inclusion for uninitiated persons some churches use screens to project the words of hymns; they avoid "in house" language in the announcements; and, the minister makes participation in worship accessible for persons lacking a church background. Ministers who care about communication use common words to explain the message, even at the expense of a longer sermon.

Post-Denominational Loyalty

Ministry today takes place in a culture lacking denominational loyalty. While older Americans are known for their loyalty to brand names, clubs, and denominations, Baby Boomers tend to value personal fulfillment over loyalty. This attitude "...means a willingness to switch to another church if [one's] needs will be met there."[10] This lack of loyalty to one's birth church creates a type of the post-denominational world. The full import of this Baby Boomer attitude toward the church will not be realized for some time. Denominations, like other institutions have a way of hanging on in spite of their ineffectiveness. They will probably continue in some configuration far into the future but quite unlike their structure in the twentieth century.

For two centuries the "mainline" denominations dominated the American religious scene — Episcopal, Presbyterian, Methodist, Disciples of Christ, United Church of Christ, American Baptist, and Lutheran, to name the major ones. For over thirty years all these denominations have been in a state of decline — for the first time since the founding of the nation. Alongside these denominations in this century alone thousands of non-denominational, charismatic, independent Bible churches have arisen. What these independent congregations will be like in the twenty-first century is not yet apparent but most likely they will form an alliance for mission and ministry.

The loss of denominational loyalty presents a new challenge for mainline churches. In the past congregations have counted on denominational loyalty, denominational financial support, and commitment to a certain denominational style. These taken-for-granted commitments of the past have gone the way of extended families and small family farms and likely cannot be counted on in the future.

The erosion of denominationalism in America has not come in a single Noahic flood, rather it has slowly eroded over the past three or four decades. Perhaps the single most important factor in the erosion of denominationalism has been the response toward the church of those persons born after 1950. These generations have not maintained loyalty to the denomination of their birth; their values conflict with those of their parents and their parent's church; and for the most part they have dropped out of church.

How can a church that promotes self-denial attract Baby Boomers committed to self-fulfillment? "The fact is that the more strongly one holds to an ethic of self-fulfillment, the less likely one is to belong to the church."[11] Their absence accounts for much of the decline in membership, influence, and financial stability of the mainline denominations.

The weakening of denominational loyalty has been exacerbated by a mobile population. With the advent of the automobile, the migration of the farm population to the city, and the regular movement of employees in major corporations, the old loyalty to one's church of birth has vanished. The automobile destroyed the regional parish by making it possible for persons to worship regularly forty or fifty miles from home. It made church shopping as easy as grocery shopping. Migration to the city offered rural people many new options; whereas the rural setting provided only one or two choices, in the city they had a dozen options. The corporate policy of transferring persons from one section of the country to another tore at denominational loyalty by accentuating short-term relationships. Persons decided on their church by the church's responsiveness to their needs and not according to their history or tradition. Since rootless families seek instant community, the friendly church wins out over the birth denomination.

Add to these influences the propensity of certain denominations, when threatened by the winds of change, to retreat into rigid traditions. When these congregations become tradition-driven rather than need-responsive to persons in the general population, they lose their former constituency. Even when many congregations were struggling for survival, the denominational bureaucracy demanded greater loyalty to the denomination. Loyalty to the institution's goals became synonymous with loyalty to Christ. These institutional emphases came at a time when the post-war generation had little regard for the tradition or for the survival of the denomination.

In addition to these negative factors that attacked denominations, another force began to emerge — the non-denominational church.[12] In almost every community in this nation this new phenomenon can be found. These congregations go by many names — Holy Spirit Chapel, Cornerstone, Christian Fellowship, Community of Love, or the Vineyard. The names indicate no denominational affiliation and the word "church" does not appear in their advertisements.

These worshipping communities respond to the felt needs of the new generation — they are need responsive. Their worship services may be characterized as less formal, with contemporary music, a high level of participation, and above all, a friendly atmosphere. These new communities of faith dot the countryside and continue to multiply; they are destined to play an influential role in the reshaping of the emerging religious scene in America.

No longer do persons consider first the denominational affiliation when selecting a church. They test the congregation for a fit with their needs and desires. Shopping for a church has become one more task in a consumer society. Even if this approach shocks our mainline religious sensibilities, it is nevertheless fact.

Fifteen years ago, Lyle Schaller said to a gathering of ministers: "By the year 2000 the largest Protestant denomination in America does not exist today!" He most likely was envisioning the confluence of the millions of non-denominational chapels and mega-churches that eventually will coalesce into denomination-like alliances.

What does it mean to evangelize in a consumer-driven, non-denominational society? The growing demand for a need-responsive church should not receive a totally negative evaluation. The pain, frustration, and hunger of persons outside the church has always mattered and still does. The damage comes when churches market the faith in a watered-down form to gain money and members. I agree with E. Stanley Ott, author of *Vision for a Vital Church*, who says, "The church must be Spirit-driven but need-responsive."[13] The church is not driven by the needs of persons but by the Spirit of Christ, yet his Spirit motivates the church to respond to the needs of persons.

Since denominational labels alone will not attract new persons, the church in a post-denominational society must give renewed attention to the authenticity of its life in Christ and always be sensitive to the expressed needs of persons within its context.

This new situation demands a clear focus on the gospel, vitality in worship, a warm, welcoming fellowship, and a profound sense of the presence of God. People visiting churches today seek a relationship with God and not a particular church's history, tradition, or governance.

A PLURALIST WORLD

The church today ministers in an increasingly pluralistic world. Christians are now one of many religious voices in Western culture and are often less aggressively missionary than devotees of other faiths, writes David Bosch. "Christians, Muslims, Buddhists, and adherents of many traditional religions rub shoulders daily."[14]

When a culture has no central authority and no shared vision of reality, it becomes fragmented with individuals holding their own relativized values. We are a culture without a central vision or an agreed upon authority for faith and morals. Our situation is reminiscent of the times of the Judges when every person was doing what was right in his or her own eyes (Judges 17:6).

A culture in which "everyone is doing what is right in his or her own eyes" gives rise to a hyper-individualism and the creation of special interest groups seeking to influence the culture according to their particular values. Perhaps Allan Bloom has rightly described our situation in *The Closing of the American Mind* when he says that the closed mind consists in the fact that we have rejected all absolutes — the only absolute principle is that all values are relative.[15]

When everything in a culture is relative, the revelation of God in Christ, the meaning of salvation, and the morals traditionally affirmed by the church can all be negotiated according to one's personal whims. In this relativized situation the Ultimate has evaporated — no tradition, no values worth sacrificing for, no great leaders or noble guides, no saints, no one who speaks with authority about the sacred dimensions of the Spirit. What an impoverished culture!

Contrast this situation with Christendom in the High Middle Ages when the church was the depository of the revelation of God and the guarantor of truth. The church guaranteed the truth of God's being the Creator and

Redeemer. From these truths the church deduced moral behavior. And, the church had the authority to enforce its interpretation at the threat of excommunication. Because the church had both ecclesiastical and political power, it could enforce its values in education, politics, the arts, and in everyday life. This power produced a synthesis that united all of life from the serf to the portals of heaven. All persons knew who they were, their places, roles, and limits.

This Medieval "ladder" of existence was dismantled rung by rung. The Reformation removed the absolute authority of the church. The Age of Revolution (during which the United States was born) undermined monarchy. And the Age of Science largely removed God from the picture. As a result, the weight of meaning has fallen heavily upon the shoulders of each individual. Thus, the pluralism, individualism, and fragmentation characteristic of the modern experience.

Not only do we find this pluralism in secular culture, it has woven itself into our religious thought. If the revelation of God in Jesus Christ has become suspect through the undermining influence of the Enlightenment and if the agreed upon center of authority and meaning has been split open by relativism, then secular persons are left to their own unaided judgment. "As the respect for the Sacred — the latest fad — has soared, real religion and knowledge of the Bible have diminished to the vanishing point."[16] In the name of freedom, in the name of respect for personhood, even Christians have become reluctant to give witness to the uniqueness and universality of Jesus Christ.

The earliest and shortest creed of the early church was "Jesus is Lord." In this confession believers confessed that in Jesus of Nazareth the living God became flesh, and through his life, death, and resurrection Christ was acclaimed the ruler of the universe. For them, Jesus was Lord of Moses, Lord of the pagan gods and goddesses, and Lord of the state. This confession made every authority subject to Jesus Christ.

The church of the twenty-first century must answer the practical question: "How do we give witness to the Lordship of Jesus Christ in a pluralistic culture?" Our inability to witness to his Lordship again raises the question, "Can our kind of church change our kind of world?"

The Christian church stands in a long, rich, historically tested tradition, affirming that God was revealed in Jesus Christ, uniquely and universally. "That God should play the tyrant over man is a dismal story of unrelieved oppression; that man should play tyrant over man is the usual dreary record of human futility; but that man should play the tyrant over God and find Him a better man than himself is an astonishing drama indeed."[17] To forsake this confession mutes the church and jeopardizes its future.

How will we do evangelism? First, we must recognize the social and political legitimacy of other religious faiths, secular faith, and no faith. In this post-modern age honesty compels us to acknowledge that we do not stand on some high moral ground from which we can speak in absolute terms to other faiths or to persons of no faith. Yet, we are Christians without apology. The scripture, the tradition, and the living church form the ground of our authority, and from this ground we give our witness. But we cannot denigrate other faiths and their revelations, traditions, and sacred practices. Good will not be served by our speaking down to others, or seeking to impose our views upon them. Convincing testimony and sincere listening will be the keys to effective evangelization.

Second, in a post-Christian age persons have the burden of choosing their center of value and the lifestyle that is shaped accordingly. On the one hand this situation affords great freedom but on the other it lays an enormous burden upon the individual. The entire weight of personal meaning rests upon the shoulders of the solitary individual — producing loneliness, anxiety, and emotional breakdown. An accepting, caring, Christian community can provide a setting and support for persons faced with this weighty task.

Third, the church and each of us believers must answer the decisive questions: "Who is Jesus Christ? And, who is Jesus Christ for me?" These questions drive to the very heart of Christian faith and life. On these confessions hang the future of evangelism and the future of the Christian church.

Fourth, the theologians of the church must help us speak about Jesus Christ in words and images that connect with life. By this I mean that we must set forth the claims of Jesus Christ in a relevant, understandable style that commends him to a broken, confused world.

Finally, we must equip persons to give witness to their faith in Jesus Christ. The equipping must be twofold: an ability to give a clear witness without being imperialistic; and the humility and the capacity to listen to those who either do not know, or do not believe the revelation of God in Christ.

Where do we go from here? Given the reality of a post-Christian, post-denominational, and pluralistic world, how will your church respond evangelistically? Several options are open:

1. Will we retreat into silence and develop our own private relationship with Christ?

2. Will we seek to maintain a magisterial position and lord it over other faiths and persons of no faith?

3. Will we settle for a shallow dialogue that makes no serious faith claims?

4. Will we begin a serious effort to translate Christian faith into understandable words and images?

5. Or, will we turn to the text and the Spirit for new images, authority, and vision for the task today?

A Liberated Imagination

The new situation demands a new way of being the church. If we are to be new and different, we must have new eyes to see; we need the freedom of a liberated imagination. The early church possessed a creative imagination that permitted it to see worship as an assembly inhabited by the risen and living Christ who met with them, filled them, and renewed their lives. "Belief in Jesus Christ — not the church, or the institution, or dogma — was the point of departure for life," says William Easum.[18] They could imagine him as a companion in the experiences of daily life. They saw his hand providentially shaping the historical occurrences of their day. And when opportunity arose, he put in their mouths words to speak, filled their hearts with compassion, and lived out his life through them. He was their method. He was their strategy.

Perhaps the twenty-first century church can become so possessed with the Spirit of Jesus Christ that it can imagine its ministry in a form that genuinely communicates the presence of the risen Lord to persons in our day.

CHAPTER 3
The People at the Door

The place of mission must once again begin "at the door" of the church. According to Acts 3:1-10 when Peter and John made their way to the temple at the hour of prayer, they encountered a beggar, lame for over forty years, lying at the door of the temple. What is the shape of mission outside the door of the post-Constantinian church? Who are the persons "outside the door" of our congregations? What are they like?

As we have seen, the context in which we minister has changed; the situation in which we evangelize has shifted; and, the persons we seek to reach are different from a few decades ago. They are different not so much in respect to their needs, but in their self-perception, their expectations, and their values. They are secular persons and their presence raises a persistent question for us: "How do we reach persons in a multi-cultural, relativistic, post-denominational, and secular world where Christianity is viewed as one of many options?" An effective ministry of outreach demands that we cast off our spectacles of prejudice and look at these persons in their context.

SECULAR PERSONS

The breakdown of Christendom gave rise to secularism with mixed benefits. Secularization freed persons from religious oppression but created a society that no longer understands itself to be Christian. Contemporary society operates with a new set of assumptions, speaks a non-religious vocabulary, judges by humanistic criteria, and embraces a variety of lifestyles. The world view of secular persons shows little contact with the Christian gospel. Because these persons do not use the Christian vocabulary to define themselves or their vision of life, George Hunter suggests a number of mythical judgments made of them.[1]

MYTHS ABOUT SECULAR PEOPLE

According to Hunter secular persons are not irreligious, bad, or sophisticated in their approach to life. The word "secular" does not mean irreligious. Secular persons born after World War II give evidence of a deep religious hunger even though it is not expressed in Christian language or lifestyle. Bookstores in shopping malls, for example, fill their shelves with books that advocate a do-it-yourself, home-made religion. These books point to religious experience as the answer to the deeper longings of the psyche. Grounded in an Eastern world view and shaped by the human potential movement, the authors of these manuals answer fundamental religious questions. They respond to every issue confronting modern persons from the nature of spiritual experience to family rituals to the preservation of the planet.

Often secular persons seek spiritual depth in disciplines like Transcendental Meditation, Zen, yoga, and physical exercise. The seriousness with which these disciplines are practiced exposes the depth of the religious hunger in persons who either have lost or never possessed a Christian grounding.

The secular religious hunger masquerades as "The American Way of Life" — civil religion. Having rejected the religion of their childhood or never having been grounded in a religious faith to reject, these Americans have placed their trust in freedom, prosperity, God, and the nation as objects of loyalty. Even though it may be an idolatrous devotion, these persons have committed themselves to "something" that offers fulfillment and promises hope for the future. People outside the door may be secular, but they have not lost their religious thirst.

Hunter states that for some persons, secular means "bad" or "immoral."[2] Such labels simply do not fit today's secular people either. Many secular persons sacrificially struggle with the great social problems facing the planet. Some have defended the unborn's right to life, while others have fought for the woman's freedom of choice. Often secular persons champion the rights of the poor and marginalized. Still other secular persons struggle for the feminists' agenda and stand up for gay liberation.

Disagreement with the positions of secular persons should not blind us to the moral depths of their passion. Such commitment stems from their essentially religious nature as human beings and perhaps the Universal Spirit, working incognito. These so-called secular persons often have a zeal for social causes akin to the bold witness of the disciples of Jesus of Nazareth. Being outside the institutional church does not silence their voices. Some secular persons live moral lives that put to shame those of many church members.

Another myth about secular persons, according to Hunter, identifies them as sophisticated religious thinkers. The myth has it that secular persons have carefully weighed the evidence for Christianity and found it lacking. According to this myth, all secular persons possess philosophical and religious sophistication. An investigation of the facts paints a different picture. According to surveys, these persons do not know the essential facts of the Christian faith, and they sometimes become gullible in their religious emptiness.[3] When secular persons are questioned about their beliefs, they often have distorted notions about crucial Christian teachings. This lack of depth, balance, and experience surfaces even in casual conversations.

A Secular Person

To dispel the myths about secular persons, talk to one. Such a conversation not only dispels the myths, but forms a sharper picture of secular individuals. I met such a person on a flight from Dallas to Atlanta.

Tim boarded the plane after I had strapped myself into my seat. He came in, took off his coat, loosened his tie, stashed his bag in the overhead compartment—like the seasoned traveler he was—and sat down beside me.

In a few moments we entered into conversation. He was a graduate of Georgia Tech and a salesman of laser surgical instruments. He was forty-odd years old, born in 1950.

He was in his second marriage; the first one lasted two years. His former wife was a flight attendant and he had married her so that he could do his business flying for only $10 per flight. A few months into the marriage his mother said, "She doesn't have much personality." That response from his mother raised a question about his good judgment.

When the newness of sex wore off, their lives settled into the routine of reading the newspaper and watching television. With devotion to work and the inability to talk meaningfully with each other, their life together soon became dull and meaningless. They got a divorce.

Resistant to making another significant commitment, he remained single for fifteen years. He then married a woman sixteen years younger than himself. She goes out with the girls while he is on the road; sometimes she goes out with her boss and customers who come to town — just part of the job.

He asked me, "What do you do?"

"Professor at a seminary."

"Sure enough?" After a pause, he added, "It's been a hard week."

"I can match it." (I was thinking of my canceled flight that afternoon and missing my birthday dinner with my wife.)

"No, you can't match my week. I've been on the road since Monday. I called my wife last night. Not in. Called until 3 a.m. Still not in. And, she wonders why I am upset. I don't know if she will be there when I get home."

"I'm sorry things have gone so badly for you. I wish I could help. As you have told me your story I have found myself wondering if you are a religious person."

"No. I used to be religious but not anymore."

"I'd be interested in knowing about that if you want to talk about it."

"I don't mind. I was raised in a church that had lots of rules. When I got away from home I learned many of those ideas were for the birds." (Actually, he used a bit stronger expression!)

"Do you think it is possible to know God?"

"Not really. There are so many religions in the world. How can any one of them claim a monopoly on God? One is about as good as another as far as I'm concerned. Besides, there are preachers like (he named one I had seen advertised in Dallas, Texas, who promised health and wealth to all who have faith) out there fleecing all those old folks. I just don't believe in it."

"What do you believe?"

"I believe that what you put into life will come back to you. I have done fairly well. I don't rip anyone off. I expect folks to treat me like I treat them."

"Tim, do you really doubt that we can know God in a personal way?"

"You may know your God, but that is for you. Mine may be very different from yours."

"Tim, if it were possible for you to know God and be in a relation with God, would you want to?"

"You can't prove God to me."

"I know I can't, but if it were possible would you?"

"Yes! Hell yes, I would like to know God."

"If you are serious about this desire, I would like to challenge you to pray every day for a month: 'O God, if there is a God, help me know that you are real!'"

"I'll do it," he said. Then he turned to me and added, "I'll tell you one thing, if this plane started down right now, I'd pray."

Here is a post-Christian, post-modern, post-denominational, secular man shaped by the values of our culture. In many ways, Tim represents the typical secular person of our day.

A Closer Look

If secular persons do not conform to our myths about them, who are they really? How are we to view those who have been shaped by the changes of our times? Talking with persons like my seat mate, Tim, helps us understand them. Additionally, Hunter has provided us with a number of helpful categories to define secular persons; George Barna has added useful research; and the social analysis of Tex Samples offers further clarification. The following categories provide further definition of secular persons.

Ignorant of the Faith

Secular people do not understand the basic affirmations of the Christian faith. This lack of understanding ranges from sheer ignorance to misinformation about the faith and includes perversions perpetuated by New Age authors and the ignorance of church members.

One young man, waiting tables at a restaurant in the Silicon Valley in California, epitomizes those who know nothing about the faith. When we met he had never been to church because before his birth his parents were betrayed by a minister and dropped out.

Others have been exposed to a form of the faith, but not to what C. S. Lewis called "Mere Christianity." These secular persons, like Tim, believe that "God helps those who help themselves." Or, as he said, "You get out of life what you put into it."

These persons need a setting in which they may learn the basics of the faith. The Christian educator must begin at the beginning, assuming that secular people know little or nothing of the faith. Donald Soper writes, "If only impassioned evangelists would tell the story of Jesus Christ, what he said, how he lived and died and what happened to those who were his disciples, if they would concentrate upon those primary elements in the Christian religion and proclaim them as if they were unfolding a new and unheard Gospel, they would over and over again be breaking virgin ground."[4] Numerous non-denominational groups have established Bible study groups offering a safe place to learn about Christian faith. They require serious study and make tough work assignments.

One particular group of secular, religious persons researchers have labeled "church dropouts." This group has also been called, "Lay Liberals"; lay, because no established theologian espouses their convictions; liberal, because they do not hold an orthodox Christian faith. These persons were born after 1950, had some minimal exposure to the church, but after college they decided the church held nothing for them. This collection of persons has dropped out of mainline churches.

What does this group of persons believe? Like most Americans they believe in God. But they also believe that all the world religions are equally good in helping persons discover Ultimate Truth. Most of them prefer Christianity but their preference lacks grounding in strong truth claims. Thus, they believe that Buddhism or Islam may be equally true for those who embrace these other faiths.

Underlying this pluralism exists the belief that a common thread of truth runs though all the great religions.

Lay Liberals view the church as supportive of a basic morality to which they want their children exposed. Though they want a moral grounding for their children, they do not talk with them about God or religious matters. These Lay Liberals do not care what faith their children embrace, only that they have the freedom to make their own choices. Regarding the future, they reject the idea of God's consigning anyone to hell; they consider reincarnation appealing, and have only vague conceptions about the fate of the soul after death.

For mainline congregations these persons provide the major reason for decline. We have lost a whole generation to the category of "church dropout." Researchers Hoge, Johnson, and Luidens challenge us: "If the mainline churches want to regain their vitality, their first step must be to address theological issues head-on. They must listen to the voices of Lay Liberals and provide compelling answers to the question, 'What's so special about Christianity?'"[5]

SELF-FULFILLMENT

According to Tex Sample, there has been a major shift in American culture from an ethic of self-denial to one of self-fulfillment. This shift toward the self has been noted by Robert Bellah and associates in *Habits of the Heart*. Bellah notes that our American belief in individualism is ambivalent. On one hand, we have no desire to return to oppressive authoritarianism. The Reformation, Enlightenment, and American Revolution have won us valued freedoms. At the same time, "modern individualism seems to be producing a way of life that is neither individually nor socially viable."[6]

The conversation with Tim, my seat-mate from Dallas, also illustrates this point. He fiercely guarded his freedom to choose, yet was deeply dissatisfied with the results of his free choices.

A few decades ago, most Americans held to the "ethic of self-denial." Self-denial found support in the Calvinist demand to deny yourself, save your money, invest it, and multiply it for future use — an ethic that fueled the capitalist economy. The ethic of "self-denial" delays gratification. It insists that we put off fulfillment now so that we may have a better future. Many of our parents held to the notion that heaven is worth whatever it costs — so endure whatever life brings to you in order to make heaven!

According to Sample, this vision of life inspired three values: sacrifice now for the sake of long-term gain; work hard so that your gain in the future may be greater; and gain the respect of the community by living out this lifestyle of self-denial.[7]

Today's secular persons have made a major shift. They are committed to the ethic of self-fulfillment. Or, as George Hunter says, they are "seeking life before death: rather than life after death."[8] Secularists have no interest in postponing gratification, but rather demand immediate gratification. A number of ingredients make up this new self-centered ethic: life has intrinsic worth. To be alive here and now provides unlimited opportunity and we should enjoy it. Affluence spawns this vision of life by giving opportunity for leisure time. Heretofore, persons were so busy surviving they had little time to ponder the value of their lives.

Secular persons want a life that is creative and emotionally expressive. They are concerned about developing their full potential. "If it feels good do it," grows out of this ethic of self-fulfillment. Feel your feelings, be in touch with yourself, live life to the fullest — are axioms of the self-expressive.

One of the best ways to reach persons seeking fulfillment is to provide groups that help them deal with their problems. Many have experienced divorce, disillusionment, some form of addiction, the emptiness of self-centered life, and emotions jaded from searching for life on the horizontal plane. The church can provide a setting for true self-fulfillment and a challenging vision for the future. The motives to which we appeal must be life-oriented. Twelve-step groups offer a place for healing and renewal. Can the church learn from this approach?

FEELINGS OF SHAME

Secular people have a greater consciousness of doubt and shame than of guilt.[9] Luther's great concern was the appeasement of the wrath of an angry God. Modern persons are unconvinced of an absolute moral standard and thus have exercised their freedom to experiment with various self-chosen behaviors which contradict Christian norms. Though these seekers for life may not feel guilt, they do often feel a deep sense of shame.

While my companion on the plane did not acknowledge his shame, I suspect that he felt some. When he spoke about his early training and the present circumstance of his life, hints of shame and regret echoed from his tone of speech. Doubt was clearly evidenced in his rejection of the church's teaching—in fact, any trustworthy religious teaching. He is a man adrift in a sea of choices.

But secular persons have also been victims of a world collapse—"meaning" has fallen in upon them and they have no certainty by which to live. Many seem to be locked up in their own consciousness with no way out of their private experiences of pleasure or pain. When persons lose their awareness of history, too much responsibility falls on the present moment — a responsibility too weighty for the individual.

Feelings of shame can be just as debilitating as feelings of guilt. Guilt refers to what one has done; shame relates to whom one fears him or herself to be.

Widespread child abuse and sexual abuse have wounded many in this generation. Confessions made public on talk shows and the proliferation of books dealing with abuse, plus support groups for abused persons indicate how widespread this destructive behavior has been. Note also that our driving need for affirmation and self-worth springs from deep feelings of shame.

NEGATIVE VIEW OF THE CHURCH

For some, the church seems hopelessly outmoded in its forms. The huge bureaucratic structure with its programs and witness leaves them cold. Too often the church appears to be primarily interested in its own survival and not in persons. This judgment of the church blocks the involvement of unchurched people.

Also, the secular person often views the church as hypocritical. The church makes a great profession but does not produce changed lives. The split between the church's words and actions costs it credibility. A cry for integrity!

To reach secular persons the church must take a hard look at itself. The hard questions it must ask include: Is our focus on church members or outsiders? Do we wish to use people to maintain the church or do we genuinely care about the pain outsiders experience? Are we more concerned with what one knows or how one serves?[10] Do we run programs or do we minister to persons?

SEPARATION

Secular people experience a great deal of alienation. Their feelings of separateness include family and friends, their work, the political process; they feel separated from nature, and even from themselves.[11] Some of them know what it means to be broken persons in a broken world.

This generation's parents divorced at a phenomenal rate; they were left with the television as a baby sitter; they moved every few years, suffering from short-term friendships. Often their work was mechanized or highly organized, robbing them of a sense of importance in the production process. All these factors combine to produce a generation of persons with deep feelings of estrangement from themselves and others.

This alienation accounts for the constant search for identity and the demand for security. The feelings of alienation feed the hunger for significant relationships. Strangely, these people who mistrust the church express a desire to be close to God.

The church must take seriously the pain of alienation that equals or surpasses Luther's anxiety over guilt and, therefore, must help persons feel part of the church and part of God's purpose in the world.

FEARFUL

Secular persons do not trust easily. Remember Tim's lack of trust. He struggled with trust in his wife of a few years, the integrity of his parents' religion, the church, and the motives of leaders. The picture of the world presented in his early church experience no longer made sense to him.

In dealing with secular persons, we must remember that for them the old certainties of God, purpose, and morals have collapsed. They have inherited a different world. Before we judge too harshly their alternative lifestyles, we should recall the stress caused by the loss of a dependable world.

A lack of trust in this generation causes them to avoid long-term commitments. A focus on today and immediate personal fulfillment forces them to look upon commitments as a threat to personal freedom.

To reach these fearful persons, the church must

demonstrate to them the love and compassion of Christ. Mead asks, "Can our congregations be seen as safe places where we can reach across boundaries...?"[12] In part, this demonstration must include a warm welcome to persons whose lives and values do not match those held by the congregation. Congregations must be havens of grace in a society characterized by aggression. Persons who have difficulty making long-term commitments require both patience and understanding.

OUT OF CONTROL

Secular persons experience the world and themselves as being out of control. The assassinations of John and Robert Kennedy, the death of Martin Luther King, Jr., the Vietnam War and the war in the Persian Gulf, along with the AIDS epidemic suggest danger and chaos. Despite the end of the Cold War, the threat of a nuclear conflict still remains a possibility. The United States lacks focus for the future; the end of the cold war has left the nation without an enemy, which forces a pseudo-unity. How deceived and manipulated must a generation feel by a government that held life in check with the threat of a nuclear holocaust!

This loss of order and control comes not only from the society or the government, it comes even closer to home. Secular persons experience their own lives as being out of control. They reflect in their personal worlds the same kind of helter-skelter confusion objectified in the larger society. Life for them lacks boundaries, direction, and securities.

With respect to evangelism, these changes challenge the church to imagine a new way of life in community that offers security and stability in a world that at best seems uncertain and at worst dangerous. Wherever a church offers genuine community and articulates a new vision of how life may be lived with meaning, the secular person will notice and seek it out.

WILLING TO TALK

Secular persons are willing to talk about their concerns and frustrations. Most persons born after 1950 have a keen awareness of both their joys and their pain. They easily identify their hopes, fears, doubts, questions, and longings. On countless talk shows these persons readily and shamelessly tell sordid stories and unmask their fear and anger. They clearly articulate their hurts and their hopes. Quite different from many of their parents who wear masks, keep secrets, and maintain a stiff upper lip.

In a 1992 television special called "Twenty-Something," journalist Barbara Walters interviewed a dozen young persons in their twenties. She explored every aspect of their lives — except religion. Interestingly, not one question about their faith was posed. These young people described concerns from family to jobs, from sex and pleasure to their diminished expectations for the future. Each new question revealed the clarity with which this generation both understands and feels its plight.

In all my encounters with unchurched persons, I have never met a person who could not converse about his or her faith or lack of it. The willingness of secular persons to talk about matters of faith catches most mainline churches at an awkward moment. Too many of us have difficulty articulating clearly a personal faith in Jesus Christ in relevant, intelligent, compelling ways. Perhaps those at the door of the church can articulate their needs more clearly than we can speak convincingly of our answers.

The most pressing challenge to the twenty-first century church may be a recovery of the language of faith. Church members must embrace the faith more fully and learn to express it in their lives. This faith must be a deep, daily trust in God, not a mere assent to Christian beliefs. Persons living their faith will find ways to communicate it.

The Challenge

As the morning of the twenty-first century dawns upon the church, it reveals the enormous challenge before us. First, these days challenge the church to examine its own life. Comparing our habitual practices to those of the early church reveals a number of glitches in our communal life. The church of today must, I believe, return to the basics of being church, to discover anew what it means to be the people of God.

Second, the church must learn how to release the multiplied energy of the laity. No longer can they content themselves with a profession of faith, church attendance, and making a financial contribution. We must once again engage the whole church in the mission.

Third, in order to reach the secular persons outside the door of the church, the typical church must face changes in its culture, its worship style, its forms of ministry, and the way it views the secular community. Without these changes nothing much will happen in our mission.

Even if these proposals create feelings of anxiety and resistance, we must change. The future depends upon it. The old ways no longer work and new ways must be born. I will make five proposals that I believe to be at the heart of the transformation that needs to occur in most mainline congregations.

PART II : THE PROPOSAL

CHAPTER 4

Proposal for a Transitional Church

Obviously, the way mainline denominations do outreach has not been working well; they have been in a state of decline for several decades. While we may be tentative about the route into the future, one must be found. This new way of life and ministry will not come through zealous reorganization, nor from complex management strategies, nor from waiting for a miracle worker, but from little innovations, tiny breakthroughs, revelations, and visions that emerge out of the faithfulness of small, vital communities of faith. Weary and frustrated church leaders will find in these renewed centers the elements of a vital church. Out of thousands of these centers, new life can erupt with church-renewing energy.

Hardly anyone believes that patching up the existing structures in congregations or denominations will bring transformation. A new era demands a new way of "doing church." Mead invites this kind of newness when he contends that "our task is no less than the re-invention of the church."[1] It cannot be renewed or revived but must be remade. Mead calls us to recover the apostolic life of the congregation and the apostolic mission that once began outside the door. He addresses head-on the lack of vision and vitality in our institutions. For too long we have equated membership with discipleship and ministry with program. In the post-Christian era we cannot pretend that every baptized member is a faithful disciple nor can we assume that every program furthers the mission of Christ.

Unquestionably Dick Junkin, former Director of Discipleship for the Presbyterian Church (U.S.A.), speaks to the same issue:

It will not be a matter of simply tinkering a bit with the form of the church we have inherited. What is called for under the present circumstances is much more thoroughgoing than this. It is "re" work that we need to do, "revisioning" or "reinventing" the church.[2]

By "reinventing" Junkin does not mean that we "create out of nothing" a new version of the church but that we must place the norms of apostolic church life in dialogue with the present context and through the inspiration of the Spirit imagine a new form of faithfulness for the present. This "re" work points to tasks that must be done again.

In the language of Old Testament scholar Walter Brueggemann we must "imagine" the life, structure, and mission of the congregation in forms that respond to the present crisis. He defines imagination as "the capacity to entertain images of reality other than those presently at hand." According to Brueggemann this kind of imagination is neither "didactic nor coercive." We cannot instruct our imagination nor can it be forced! But we can open ourselves to the Spirit who inspires spontaneous visions of new possibilities that are inwardly compelling. Through the Spirit the early church possessed this creative imagination and spiritual power that enabled it to imagine the church as the Body of Christ, a community through which Jesus continued his mission.

REINVENTION REQUIRED

Every mainline denomination contains thousands of congregations that lack vitality, vision, growth, and effective mission. The setting of these congregations varies. They can be found in almost every location — rural, small town, urban, suburban, and inner-city. Many have existed in the same location since about the turn of the century. The context has changed — the geography is different, new kinds of people have moved into the neighborhood, land has been developed, houses and businesses need repair — to name a few of the changes.

Within the congregation changes have also been occurring: the membership has been declining for thirty years, the average age of members exceeds 50 years, the church school is heavily weighted with middle and older adults. The form of worship shows few changes over the last quarter century and attendance has dropped drastically from the late 1950s and early 1960s. Programs have shrunk with the loss of membership and income. Budget increases have been achieved with inflated dollars and sacrificial giving by fewer persons. Outreach to new persons has often been motivated by the church's concern for survival; the aim has been new member recruitment, not personal transformation. The congregation has witnessed the baptism of a few children and youth but hardly any adult baptisms in recent memory. The values, visions, and lifestyles of the members replicate those of the culture at large.

The attitude of the congregation has turned toward survival. The fear of extinction has created conflicting goals — reach new people, protect the church by holding onto tradition. This split mentality becomes self-defeating by excluding the very persons the church desperately wants and needs. New ideas, innovations, and changes meet with rejection for fear they will hasten the demise of the congregation; furthermore, the changes do not serve the needs of the longtime members.

Congregations with these characteristics need to do the "re" work — revision, revitalization, renewal. Without re-visioning their life and mission they are doomed to decline and eventual extinction. Admittedly, not every congregation in these declining denominations faces the threat of extinction. Some congregations through a tough management style and a strong marketing ability have kept the membership stable if not growing and the finances on the rise. Although these congregations probably will last into the twenty-first century, many believe that the cultural Christianity they embody will not have staying power in a radically secular and pluralistic world.

TOWARD FUTURE CHURCH

While some church reconstructionists have proposals for the shape of the church in the twenty-first century,[3] we are not so sure that success patterns in the age of transition can be extended boldly into the future; neither can these proposals be uncritically embraced by mainline congregations. In response to the demand for "reinventing" the church, we would be wise to think of this era as a period of transition from "what is" to "what is to be."

In the time between the demise of the established church until the birth of Future Church, we must do our "re" work — revision, revitalization, renewal. This kind of work will produce a "transitional church" in which we return to the basics of "being church," being the Body of Christ. If the transitional church effectively bridges from the present into the future, it must turn with renewed concern toward God; it must find ways to deepen authentic relationships between God and persons and among persons; it must turn outward in compassion and service through a vital membership weekly renewed through the worship of God.

None of us knows the shape of Future Church but a church that manifests the character of the apostolic church will find fruitful ways to live and witness in an alien culture. To assist the Constantinian church to move through the transitional church phase I propose five initiatives: recover a sense of the presence of God, create small groups of vital disciples, shift ministry from maintenance to mission, revitalize worship, and liberate the laity. Each of these initiatives, if successful, will precipitate change in present day congregations — change in vitality, change in witness, change in outreach, and change in vision. We remain uncertain as to what new form these changes will ultimately lead. In various forms these five initiatives already bring new life to numerous congregations, and as struggling churches move in these directions, new life will begin to appear.

RECOVERING A SENSE OF THE PRESENCE OF GOD

The church is the people of God; God lives in the midst of the people. The church is the Body of Christ; he lives in and ministers through his body. The church lives and ministers in the confidence of his promises: "I will not leave you orphaned; I am coming to you. (My Father and I) will come to them and make our home with them" (John 14:18,23).

The New Testament church lived in an amazing sense of the divine presence. They believed that Christ was in them, manifesting his life to them in their gatherings, guiding them in their work, and continuing his ministry through them. They called this presence, "Holy Spirit."

There has been an erosion of confidence in the presence of God in the church. In place of this core conviction of presence, in recent years we have substituted bureaucracy, management, the therapeutic, and tradition. These substitutes for the divine presence have failed:

☀ *Bureaucracy* — "Someone up there in the structure really knows what is going on and will 'fix things' if we just give the money." FAILED!

☀ *Management* — "All we need for the revitalization of the church is a set of goals, objectives, and strategies." FAILED!

☀ *The therapeutic* — "The real problems of the church can be solved with the transformation of the mission so that it addresses our insecurities and neuroses." FAILED!

☀ *Tradition* — "If we cling to the 'old ways' but do them better and with greater confidence, they will work." FAILED!

One way we prepare our consciousness to receive the gift of the presence of Christ is through prayer. Prayer marks our acknowledgment of authority over us; prayer is the posture of a church that believes God to be the source of its life. Prayer opens the community to God, to the Mystery incomprehensible, to the Holy unapproachable. An encounter with the Holy Spirit transforms us at the core of our being — making us new and empowering us with vision and energy for Christ's mission in the world.

Vital worship also renews our sense of the divine presense.

Vital worship and divine presence have an inseparable mutuality. True worship by definition focuses on the presence of God; there can be no experience of the Holy God that does not evoke the spirit of worship in the community. The presence of God in worship always comes to us as a gift, but attitudes and postures like prayer, expectancy, and silence prepare the community for the divine visitation. Perhaps more than anything else the practice of silence would help many mainline congregations recover a sense of the divine presence.

A VITAL CORE OF COMMITTED DISCIPLES

Congregations need a vital core of committed disciples. Certainly Christ calls the whole membership to vital discipleship, but the transformation of the Constantinian church requires a beginning point. To move from a Constantinian church to an apostolic church will not be achieved in one giant step. Mammoth changes occur bit by bit. These incremental changes can best begin with one small group of twelve or twelve groups of twelve that seek to become serious, committed followers of Jesus Christ. These disciples will both know and model the faith. This group or cluster of groups will become leaven for the whole congregation.

What will these groups do? Dick Junkin, former director of discipleship for the PC(USA), has identified six practices of these small, intentional groups: prayer together, sharing joys and struggles, reading the scriptures to listen for the voice of God, understanding the context for ministry, discerning a call, and engaging in mutual ministry. These vital groups must be grounded in prayer; prayer that offers praise and thanksgiving to God and prayer that places before God the needs of the world; and, prayer that prepares us to discern the presence of God. Open sharing of faith and life provides the framework for the birth of community, and without it the group cannot survive. Note that these groups read scripture to listen for God to speak. The text mediates the word of God to the group.

Prayer, sharing, and scripture reading nurture the life of the group but the vision does not end with intimate, joyous fellowship. These groups aim to understand the needs of the community outside their fellowship, discern the call of God to them, and get involved in the service of humankind. According to Junkin, the key to discernment is found in the pain of the people.

These six spiritual practices may not be those that you would assign to groups of vital disciples. Make your own list of disciplines informed by scripture and inspired by the Spirit. At a minimum this vital core of disciples must open themselves to study scripture, share life together, pray, and engage in the mission of Jesus Christ. Is this not what Christians have always done?

These vital groups will function in three ways: give strength and encouragement to the pastor, provide a place for new persons to meet God, and give birth to a new kind of leader.

Increasingly ministers find themselves the target of criticism, false judgment, and suspicion. Many members of the church mistrust their ministers and rail against them for their imperfections. In addition to the hostility of lay leaders, fellow clergy act destructively against each other. Even if some ministers fail to function effectively, no human being deserves the ruthless attacks and betrayals befalling many clergy today. Not every ordained minister suffers this pain and not every church spews hostility upon the clergy, but it happens too often and to too many!

The discipleship group provides the minister a source of support and encouragement. It offers a community of fellowship in which the members listen to the minister's confessions, pray for him or her, and affirm the worth of the servant of Christ. Without a supportive community many ministers suffer defeat, frustration, and loss of hope.

Second, this vital group will provide a place for new persons to experience the faith. I fear that many of our role models only prove effective in producing staggering Christians. We are producing more persons like ourselves! Instead of dynamic, enthusiastic disciples, most new members acclimate to the nominally religious life of the congregation. Too many congregations lack the power to transform secular persons (or, for that matter their own membership) into dynamic disciples. Some even lack the interest to help new persons "know the Lord" and the Lord's will for their lives.

Suppose a visitor at one of our churches shamelessly confessed, "I'm looking for God." How would we respond to this serious seeker? Too many, we fear, would say, "Join our church. Attend the services. Give your money. Serve when called upon." These directives assume that participation provides a transformation that results in knowing God. Unfortunately this model works quite well! It produces more members like those we already have.

I recommend the small, vital group as a place to discover faith. When persons come searching for spiritual vitality we should be able to introduce them to a small group appropriate to their needs. In this intimate setting they begin to understand the Christian faith and how to live as a disciple of Jesus. In this fellowship the searching person hears other lay persons pray, share real struggles, and read scripture. In this microcosm of the church they learn about ministry and discernment. In short they catch the Spirit of Christ from others and find support and direction for living the faith.

The new generations returning to the church for a second look hope to find an experience of Christ that has integrity and authenticity. They have no interest in the church as an institution; supporting or maintaining the existing structure has not made their list of values. So when they come to the church requesting baptism for a child, counseling, or help with personal issues, we must meet them at the point of their need. And, especially when they inquire about Jesus Christ or God or the experience of faith, we must respond to their questions and fears with clarity and conviction. The worst possible scenario depicts hungry people coming to the table and finding it bare, coming for a word of hope and hearing doubt or despair, or worse, silence.

To this need for spiritual direction and nurture the vital group of serious disciples also provides an answer. When persons come to the church inquiring about God, the meaning of life, or spiritual experience, the church has a place to invite them to discover faith. In the fellowship of this group, persons will receive acceptance, love, and a listening ear; in this setting they can shamelessly ask their deepest questions and find answers.

As seeking persons feel the warmth of this burning faith, they will be encouraged to get closer, to risk more, and even catch the spirit of faith. As they continue to participate in this vital community of faith they will become aware that changes are occurring. Perhaps they will even make decisions about their lives that will change both their direction and devotion. Later on they will talk about their discoveries; they will share new insights as those who have come alive from death; and, they will participate in the mission of the group as God calls them. Because of the new life they experience, they will soon invite friends to participate in the church and to test out the small group as a place for their own spiritual discoveries. This process of transformation and sharing depicts the contagious life of the congregation as it ought to be!

Third, these intentional groups will train a new type of leader. For several decades mainline congregations have struggled with mediocre lay leadership by installing nominal Christians as church leaders. Too often these persons have been made leaders in the church because they give generously, have status in the community, or have been successful in a career or business. None of these attributes alone validates them for leadership of the people of God. The church has also chosen leaders for their expertise in developing goals and objectives and strategies in industry. One does not need to know God nor be committed to Jesus Christ to excel in managerial leadership. A transitional church cannot afford to follow an uncommitted leadership no matter how successful these persons may have been in business nor how much they contribute to the budget. The church of Jesus Christ is "dying" for committed leaders.

These persons in small groups—with whom the pastor prays, listens to the voice of God, and seeks God's will and presence in ministry—will have their notions of leadership shaped by these experiences, in contrast with the traditional selection of leaders on the basis of their standing in the community. In the small group they will define the Christian life as consisting of prayer, fellowship, nurture, and mission. The group becomes their school to learn how to live a faithful life — a source of encouragement when they fail. Life together in this community begins to define how the church should function. As the congregation notices the changed lives of these persons and their deep involvement in the mission of Christ, these men and women will be called forth as leaders. In those roles, their concept of the nature and mission of the church and how the church should live out its obedience will have been informed by small group life. These persons will become a new breed of leader in the church.

Shift from Maintenance to Mission

Most mainline congregations require a shift from a "maintenance" mode to a missional mode. The change in mind-set regarding mission will deliver these congregations from a fixation on the past and engage them with the new demands of their present environment. Furthermore, this change will break their preoccupation with mere survival, a malady that stifles growth and stiffens resistance to change.

Far too many mainline churches are being consumed with maintenance requirements—perhaps as many as 75 or 80 percent. Before exploring the missionary perspective, consider the properties of a maintenance-minded congregation. First, it is controlled by an orientation toward the past; they tend to recall the "good old days" of the Eisenhower church when attendance and membership peaked. Congregations trapped in a maintenance mentality defend against change; resisting change protects traditional practices. Decline also characterizes the congregation given to maintenance; it has been losing members slowly for the last 30 years and now enjoys only a third to half its previous membership. Along with all these characteristics the maintenance church opts for the status quo; it tends to keep both programs and structures in place, almost revering them as sacred.

Resistance to change eventually blinds this congregation. This self-inflicted blindness causes leaders not to see what has taken place in their immediate environment. They seem not to notice that new and different people have moved into the vicinity of the church; they discount the fact that a shopping center has taken the place of a corn field; they ignore the evidence of deteriorating houses. In their blindness these congregations live with an illusion: if we do what we have always done, except better and with greater zeal, we will eventually get back to where we once were. Unconsciously, they delude themselves that the "way things used to be" is the "way things ought to be."

The way into the future is no mystery. This church can change; it can become an authentic representation of Jesus Christ; it can have vitality and life — if it is willing to pay the price! First, this church requires a vision of the future. This means that the focus of attention must shift from past to future. This shift will liberate the congregation from a past-orientation and it will destroy the illusion that the past can be resurrected in the present.

What must go into this vision? Three simple ingredients: a vision is inspired by the Spirit from an encounter with the text of scripture, in the present geographical and social context. The vision will be limited only by resources of persons and funds. So the chaos over which the Spirit broods to create vision are text, context, and resources.

The people of God must open their eyes to the context. Most of our declining congregations are situated in a socially or economically different context from where they were thirty or forty years ago. A different social, economic, and cultural group of people has moved into the environs of the church. What appealed to the former residents does not appeal to the new ones. For congregations to be effective, they must learn to minister to a different kind of constituency.

Finally, the people of God must embrace a realistic vision expressive of their potential. Every church has a limited amount of money and people to invest in mission. Of course, that limit is not nearly so small as most of us think. We can give more and do more than we imagine but ultimately these two resources limit the extent of our mission.

The maintenance mentality will be transformed into a missional vision when the congregation decides to risk change. The courage to risk change comes from the congregation's decision to place its trust in God to lead them into the future.

Revitalize Worship

The revitalization of worship may be the single most important challenge the transitional congregation faces. Most worship services need a change in form, style, language, and music.

The absurdity of conducting worship in one culture while trying to minister to persons of a very different culture struck me while worshipping in a Reformed congregation in Johannesburg, South Africa. The vast majority of persons in the service had come to Johannesburg from numerous African countries and, for the most part, were black. The language, liturgy, and music had not changed since it was imported from Scotland more than ten decades before. An organ provided the music, the hymns were unfamiliar to me and to most of those present, and the language for the most part appealed to a European audience rather than to Africans who struggled under the oppressive system of apartheid. The form of the service had no grounding or relevance in the culture of the participants. Maybe it was easier for me to recognize the incongruity in another setting than it would be to critique my own congregation's relevance to persons born after 1950.

Perhaps an outsider could go into most of our churches and identify the archaic ways in which we worship — unintelligible forms, obscure language, and music from another time and place. Whether invited or not, members of the "Boomer Generation" make these assessments of our worship when they return to church. They look at our order of worship, listen to our music, wonder about our language, and conclude, "Just like it was before I left" and then leave again. If congregations are serious about reaching the "lost generation" and their children, they must examine their worship.

Worship focuses on "the praise of God." Worship need not be confused with showing off one's dress, nor attracting new persons, nor advocating causes, nor even with teaching or evangelizing. Worship focuses on God! It aims first at the praise of God. Other benefits may accompany worship when it proves alive and relevant — pageantry, evangelism, instruction, and edification — but we cannot afford to make the focus of worship anything other than the glory of God.

THE FORM OF WORSHIP

By form we mean the shape of the liturgy. Every church from Pentecostals to Roman Catholics has a liturgy. Liturgy comes from the Greek word meaning "work," the work of the people of God in the worship of God. The order for "the work of the people" must be appropriate for the persons doing the work. Persons who have been schooled in a classical liturgy of the Lord's Day in a particular tradition consider it the proper order of worship. But persons enculturated in a less formal, more spontaneous order consider theirs to be the correct form. And, then there are those persons with no previous experience of worship who understand neither the classical forms nor the spontaneous ones. If we hope to reach new people, our liturgy must be accessible to them.

Having a different or a simple liturgy does not mean that liturgy must insult human intelligence or divine holiness. Good liturgy enables people to offer praise and worship to God. In a secular age we must be prepared for persons who understand nothing about the church's traditional liturgy. For example, a university graduate attended worship and afterward asked the pastor, "What were you doing with that bread and wine this morning?"

The task for many congregations today is examining the form of their worship from the perspective of an outsider. Changes can be made that do not compromise the integrity of worship but which make worship accessible to those persons unfamiliar with the traditional ways.

THE STYLE OF WORSHIP

The style of worship denotes the manner in which it is conducted as well as the way persons participate. Perhaps the terms "formal" and "informal" point to this distinction. Formal worship suggests the setting of a gothic cathedral with robed choirs, ministers with vestments, sermons read in a 'stained glass' voice, accompanied by stiff movements in the pulpit, with no references to the person of the preacher nor to the lives of the people in the pews. The posture and the participation of the congregation mirrors the rigidity of the minister.

Informal worship evokes the image of reverence in a casual style. For example, the service may be conducted in a fellowship hall without hymnals, using transparencies to project song lyrics onto a screen; keyboards, guitars, and horns provide the music in place of an organ. Participants dress casually in jeans and sport shirts, and the fellowship exudes warmth and welcome. The service does not follow a printed bulletin nor does it have ushers or choirs.

Often the minister models the worship style. When the bulletin is carefully followed, the sermon read from a manuscript, and the worshipers sense that the focus of the service rests on someone other than themselves, the service loses the feeling of urgency and intimacy. Nothing much happens between the minister and the people or between the people and God. By contrast when ministers have a conviction that they are speaking for God and address the congregation with the expectation that God will speak to persons, the encounter is filled with transformative power.

THE LANGUAGE OF WORSHIP

Not only must the form of worship become accessible to outsiders, it must also be in a language they can understand. Those who plan worship should remember that many persons who visit do not know the language of faith. Care should be taken so that the language of the liturgy, the hymns, and the sermon communicate with all present.

Special attention should be given to the language of the sermon. Words like "grace," "communion," and "reconciliation" commonly used in worship may have little or no meaning to persons without a church background. A short phrase or explanation woven into the sermon can make these theological terms accessible to visitors. What virtue can be ascribed to sophisticated sermons when the hearers do not understand them? Biographers say that John Wesley read his sermons to the maid before preaching them to a wider group of people. If there was a single word she did not understand, he changed it — not preaching any sermon to others until she understood every word.

THE MUSIC OF WORSHIP

Finally, the music. Does the music of your church communicate the message of the gospel to those who attend worship? Would it communicate with a younger generation? The younger generation does not listen to the music of Bach, Beethoven, and Brahms. Classical music represents only 2 percent of the music sold in America. Yet, classical music represents about 98 percent of music played in church. Most unchurched persons do not listen to classical music. They listen to rock, jazz, and fusion created on keyboards, guitars, brass, and drums. Their music has a beat foreign to most churches.

Congregations that reach the majority of persons born after 1950 offer the gospel through music this generation understands and appreciates. Moreover, the liturgy is accessible, and the songs are simple with repetitive words and chords. The music of most mainline churches does not communicate with the marginal; it is like a foreign tongue they have never studied.

LIBERATE THE LAITY

In the early church all shared in the ministry; each possessed a gift and each a function in the Body of Christ. The false elevation of the clergy to a position of authority and dominance instead of one of service created a chasm between the ordained and the unordained. The Constantinian church exacerbated the distinction between two types of members. Even though the "priesthood of all believers" provided a plank in Luther's Reformed platform, the laity have never received full status in the church. Consequently, the laity have remained second class citizens in the church, unacknowledged as ministers of God in their secular vocations. Even John Calvin's emphasis on the worldly vocation of the laity has lacked power in any sustained form to restore a sense of divine call to the workplace. Too often, the only image of authentic ministry in the mind of the lay person is that of the ordained pastor.

Future Church cannot continue to function as the domain of the ordained minister but must find ways to liberate the laity to participate fully in the ministry of Christ. In these days of transitional congregations, churches in the "former" mainline should begin setting laity free to participate in the leadership of the congregation, to show ministries of compassion, to provide mentorship, and to embrace their "worldly calling" as the call of Jesus Christ to minister through their daily work.

HOPE FOR THE FUTURE

Is there hope for the future? Yes! Not hope in our power to reform and restructure the church but hope in God. Our God can bring life out of death, newness out of decay, and light out of darkness. We must put our hope in God.

I once had a Yucca Plant in my office, though I am not too attentive to plants. We travel in the summer and leave the plants to fend for themselves. Most of them die. Such was the fate of the Yucca plant.

The leaves died and the stalk rotted. It showed no sign of life. Once I squeezed the bark and it spewed dust in my face. It was dead — dead — dead.

Then Nan, my wife-secretary, began pouring cold coffee in the pot. Since we do not have a lavatory in the office, the pot in which this dead plant stood became the receptacle for leftover coffee, stale water, and warm Coke.

One day I noticed a peculiar thing. There was a green sprout about the size of my thumb nail growing out of the ground next to the dead trunk. This gave me hope! Maybe this plant was not dead. So I began to water it with pure water. The thumb sized leaf multiplied until there were eight leaves draping over the lip of the pot.

"Son of Man, can these bones live again?"

Indeed, because God brings life out of death!

PART III: THE PRAXIS

CHAPTER 5

How to Reorient the Congregation

To see a congregation shift from a maintenance mode to a missional mode requires time and patience. Especially patience. After four years of serious work we have seen the mentality of our congregation begin to make significant shifts.

This congregation has had years of good pastors; we were not a wounded church nor a divided church. For the past 30 years the membership declined about 30 percent, grew older, and the facilities showed signs of wear. Programs were recycled year after year. We were a typical maintenance congregation. Stories abounded about the past pastors, programs, and achievements but there were no stories about the future.

As we began a new chapter in ministry, we chose to become a vital congregation yet knowing that vitality is always the gift of God. Instead of a dull, boring, lifeless church, we wanted to be a vigorous, need-responsive family of God making a humble attempt through our ministry to reach as many persons as possible.

To become this kind of church required us to look at our concept of mission. Mission does not mean opening a food pantry or adding a day care program; it demands a whole new way of looking at ministry. We chose as our purpose, "helping people to grow in their love for and service to God, the church, and the world." Everything we do is measured by this purpose. The process for achieving this goal is defined as "vital signs."

Every ministry must be marked by these signs: Spirit-driven, Bible-based, Discipleship-directed, Need-responsive, Gathered for nurture and Scattered for service, Principle-patterned, and Reflectively-Practiced.[1] We bring this perspective on the purpose and process of ministry to every- thing we do; if it does not achieve this purpose, we don't do it.

With patience and persistence we have begun to experience significant changes in our ministry together. Should you visit us on Tuesday night you might see six people using the office phones, making the monthly contact with every family in the congregation, our tele-care ministry. If you came on Sunday morning, you would find special parking places for visitors; you would be met in the parking lot by parking lot ushers to help you feel welcome. In worship you would feel a spirit of hospitality; you would experience the pace and rhythm of the service as creative and restorative.

On Wednesday evening you would meet a short-term mission group working on language skills or see Stephen ministers being equipped for works of compassion; you would see fellowship groups meeting. All these sessions equip mem- bers and send them into their homes, their work, and their community to do ministry.

A quick evaluation reveals that we are a high commitment church. We ask people to attempt big things and we give them generous support. The transformation that we have begun to experience has required a different orientation for the whole congregation. We have been careful to honor the past while moving into new ways of ministry. We have recruited leaders who committed significant blocks of time and energy to make us a vital church. These shifts in perspective have changed the role of the pastor from chaplain to leader.

Not only have we begun to experience a change in our vision for ministry, numerous individual lives are being transformed. I think of the change a man in his thirties experienced during a mission trip to Costa Rica; a widow who has become one of the most articulate Bible teachers I have ever known; a couple who joined a small group and found a new depth in their relation to Christ and each other; a business man who is taking love and compassion into a cut-throat world; numerous families who are practicing faith in their homes and at table worship.

After six years we have turned some important corners in shaping our ministry in new ways. Strength in a congregation increases when a vital concept of ministry is applied over a long period of time. At first I felt alone with this approach to ministry because the changes did not occur overnight. But today I am supported by this congregation and it is an exciting place to do ministry because more and more members are catching the vision. We increasingly believe that this is not a "once" or a "future" church. It is a church for today! To God be the glory! (INTERVIEW WITH E. STANLEY OTT, PASTOR, PLEASANT HILLS COMMUNITY PRESBYTERIAN CHURCH, PITTSBURGH, PA.)

This call for a "new church" to minister in a "New Day" focuses on three aspects of effective ministry — The Context, The Proposal, and The Praxis. In this Praxis section we will provide clear guidance to a congregation desiring to implement the proposals made to mainline congregations. None of these proposals is novel; each calls the church back to essential practices — prayer, fellowship, worship, and mission through a liberated laity. These foundation stones must be laid anew if we are to move confidently into the future.

We have proposed the critical change in mission orientation, a shift from maintenance to mission. The interview with E. Stanley Ott, pastor of a growing mainline congregation in Pittsburgh, illustrates such a shift. To make this shift a congregation must overcome the blocks to change — past orientation, defensiveness, protection of the status quo, blindness to change, and illusions that the past can be resurrected. We have no need to destroy nor even devalue the past; perhaps it was good for the time. But today the church cannot minister as though the setting has remained the same as a few decades ago; it must adjust to its new context.

> For a congregation to have integrity today, it must embody the presence of Christ in a changed context and faithfully carry out his mission. Nothing less will suffice.

Calling the church to prayer, developing vital mission groups, revitalizing worship, and liberating the laity opens the church and its members to the presence of Christ. Faithful pastors and liberated laity who discern their calling to minister both within the church and the community participate in Christ's mission. In this chapter we will introduce a process that will help a particular congregation to begin the shift from a maintenance to a missional posture.

Since we do not know the form of Future Church, we are calling for a "transitional church." The present-day established church will become the transitional church before the emergence of Future Church (the re-formed church). Movement toward a vital, relevant "Future Church" requires bold initiatives. The following initiatives offer constructive ways to begin the transformation:

First, review the present program and practices of your congregation. These include the program, process, context, and identity of your congregation.[2]

Examine the *program* of your congregation. Identify all the ministry efforts presently being conducted. Classify the congregation's ministry in two groups: to members or to the unchurched. What are the unmet needs in these two spheres of ministry? The call to mission arises in response to the needs of persons. The discernment of need will eventually emerge through the mission groups, but in the transitional era these needs may be identified and suggested by the governing body.

Evaluate your ministry from the perspective of your mandate "to make disciples of Jesus Christ." Do your members help persons to grow in love for God, the church, and the World?[3]

Examine the *process* of ministry in your congregation. How does the congregation get its work done? Note who does the work, the manner in which the work is done, how members relate to each other, and how decisions are made. Is your work done in a nurturing environment? As you develop mission groups, begin to shift to them both the ministry to persons within the church and to needs outside the congregation. Move away from programs that come from the top down and require extended supervision and encouragement. The transitional church should define its mission through communal discernment nurtured with prayer, scripture study, and worship.

Analyze the *context* of ministry. Context refers to setting, the situation for ministry. Where is the congregation carrying out its mission? Identify all the external forces and influences affecting the congregation's mission. The *needs of persons in our context* awaken our calling along with the Spirit's ministry in the faith community.

Define your *identity*. Who are you as a church? What is significant about your name? What is your address? Describe your constituency. What mixture of memories, values, and histories give your congregation its unique identity? You can discover this identity by collecting the perceptions of those within the congregation, but the images which outsiders maintain about your church also will be of importance.

Your self-perception and the perception of others forms your identity.[4]

ORIENT THE CONGREGATION

Engage the congregation in evaluating its ministry.

1. Set forth the current program, process, context, and identity of the congregation — the result of research suggested in the foregoing paragraphs.

2. Review membership trends over the past 20 years. How do you account for the changes?

3. Study the first four chapters of this text to help the congregation understand the reasons for change.[5]

4. The pastor(s) must give leadership in analyzing the congregation, defining the mission, establishing priorities, and equipping the leaders. Unless pastors provide vision and grow with the people, they will be unable to give leadership in congregational renewal.

5. While conducting this research into congregational life, launch an emphasis on prayer. An environment of prayer will empower new decisions. See Chapter 7 for Help in beginning groups.

TIPS ON THE CHANGE PROCESS

Anticipate resistance to change and be prepared to respond to it. A discussion of the different forms of resistance may help you anticipate some of the reactions. A number of factors like tradition, form, distribution of power, and a survival mentality combine to make change difficult for the church.

Tradition. Most congregations have a long, rich, and valued tradition. Changing "the way things have always been" devalues history and calls into question sacrifices made to establish the church. Yet, clinging to the past leads to death; the past can only be honored and preserved by fusing it with the present.

Power. Generally, small congregations have a narrow base of power. Often a few families control crucial decisions by their accumulated influence or by the threat to withdraw financial support. These few persons dictate the ministry, form, and future of the church. Help these persons to see that sharing power multiplies power rather than decreasing it. Unless this restrictive control is broken the congregation will suffocate.

Form. Every congregation has established ways of doing ministry. These include the forms of worshipping, making decisions, sharing information, and relating to each other. Challenging an established form sometimes threatens long-time members. Forms create security and identity for older members, and making changes creates fear and uncertainty. Wise leaders will explain "why" changes are necessary and initiate them gradually.

Small Groups. Some congregations, especially small ones, do not feel the need for small groups — since they reason that they are a small group. Small groups that offer community and support appeal to a mobile, rootless generation. Don't pressure persons who have the support of an extended family to participate in small groups. Invite marginal persons and new persons who feel a need for this grounding. They will welcome the opportunity to be known and to feel included. When small groups begin to function effectively, provide an opportunity for longtime members to listen to the stories of new persons in the church. These testimonies will help them better understand persons unlike themselves.

Survival. When congregations become fixated on survival, they experience new persons as a threat. Survival-oriented congregations experience any challenge to the status quo as "the enemy." Since new people bring new needs and new ideas and do not honor the mores of the church, they often meet with rejection ("We don't do it that way" or "We have already tried that and it failed"). This unintended rejection quickly drives new persons to the margin of the church. Quite unconsciously this survival mentality becomes counterproductive by expelling the very persons so necessary for the congregation's future.

Why Change? Congregations must deal with persons who cannot see the value of change. The church has served them well for a number of years; why interrupt their peace of mind? For them the risk exceeds the reward. These saints of God must be helped to see that the church extends beyond their life and that they must leave a healthy community for their successors.

Some congregations resist becoming multi-cultural — that is, bringing different kinds of persons into the church. Many mainline congregations are becoming increasingly homogeneous. If this class-bound, mainline church expects to survive, however, it must welcome different kinds of people. Small groups offer the most effective way to loosen the stricture at the entry-way.

Though diversity is necessary, white, educated, upper-class congregations have problems welcoming persons of a different social class. Persons from the margins of society feel ill at ease in a large group of affluent people. Yet the insiders and outsiders can meet and relate to each other in a small group setting. When they have become friends in the small group, group members host them as they attend worship and other gatherings of the church.

Changing congregations face these challenges. The stakes are high. Either the church changes or it dies!

EXPEL THE GHOSTS OF THE PAST

Expel the ghosts of the past that haunt the memories of longtime members. Those persons who have been members for twenty or thirty years recall another era when the church was quite different. They cherish memories of full choirs, packed sanctuaries, and the good will and interest of the general population. While the heyday of this Constantinian church reached its peak in the late 1950s, the memory of those days of glory remain the ideal for the church today. Yet we cannot possibly recover the past. Even the most adept leaders cannot recreate the old situation. Nevertheless, many in the church still demand of the clergy these signs of success.

Perhaps nothing is more important for the transitional church than getting rid of the notion that the post-war boom in church attendance, building, and giving was the high water mark in the life of the church. Many scholars believe the seeming success of churches in the 1950s exemplifies the cultural success of the Constantinian church more than a manifestation of apostolic Christianity. Since the congregation cannot return to the past, and even the desire to do so is questionable, it must rediscover its life, its reason for being, and its new role in a new day. Could it be that disillusionment with the Constantinian church will provide the impetus for a rebirth of the apostolic mission?

EFFECTIVE PRINCIPLES OF CHANGE

These principles of change identified by Loren Mead will assist your church in moving into the future.[6] Because none of us knows the exact shape of Future Church, a transitional church must ground itself in the basics of the church's life. As prayer, small group life, vital worship, and lay ministry begin to take shape, numerous issues of change will require resolution. These congregationally tested principles can provide helpful guidance:

1. *Look for change opportunities.* Each congregation has particular seasons when it is more open to change. These may include the calling of a new pastor, the death of a prominent member, a catastrophe like a fire, a major economic change, or change in the context. When the anticipated future no longer seems possible, persons are willing to consider an alternative. Timing often spells success or failure of any plan.

2. *Cast changes in the mode of an experiment.* Most congregations will try new forms of ministry if they have

assurance that change may not be permanent. Try new ventures, evaluate, get feedback from the congregation, and integrate the learnings into the life of the congregation. In the proposed structure of prayer, small groups, revised worship, and lay involvement, each should be introduced as an experiment, an innovative response to the changing culture. Give these experiments strong leadership for a sufficient time to produce valuable insights and desired changes. Share both successes and failures with the congregation.

3. *Pay attention to boundaries.* Persons face difficulty in crossing from one culture into another. The Alban Institute first recognized this principle while studying the transition of ministers from the seminary culture into the culture of a particular church. As with the minister's moving from the known to the unknown, such changes invite a congregation to move out of a comfortable, known culture into an unfamiliar culture. While these changes in congregational life make it easier for outsiders to transition into the church, they create problems for those accustomed to the more traditional form. Change always requires crossing boundaries and leaders will do well to keep in mind the tension, discomfort, and resistance to crossing them.

4. *Hold steady.* Today's urgent situation will not respond to a quick fix; it requires time. Some persons will be fascinated with the proposal for a return to basics; it will resonate with their longings, but they will need patience to see these small innovations bring transformation to the congregation. Institutions have been decades, even centuries, in their formation and a few initiatives will not lead to instant success. Prepare to invest energy and effort for an extended period of time.

5. *Build accountability into your plan.* We encourage innovation; we believe in experiment; we support those who are willing to take risks. But all innovations must have accountability. This means that lay pastors, mission groups, ministries of compassion, and pastors must be

accountable to each other, to the people, and to governing bodies. Congregations must also be accountable to the denomination. None of us represents the whole church. We belong to the Body of Christ and because we are only part of the whole, we must make ourselves accountable.

6. *Build bridges and seek allies.* The journey into the future will be lonely and frightening for pastors and congregations if they choose to "go it alone." Seek other congregations engaged in experimentation; identify other pastors seeking new forms of the church. Forge alliances with them. God's people receive strength from sharing joys and sorrows on the journey.

7. *Value failure.* Persons who never fail never try anything. A good axiom for congregations: Expect to fail in some ventures. What seems to be a failure can only be labeled such if we learn nothing from it. Learn from failures and rob them of their sting.

ADMONITIONS TO A CHANGING CONGREGATION

Working at the task of renewing congregations for more than thirty years has produced in me a variety of experiences and a few insights that may be helpful as we enter this transitional period in the life of mainline churches:

1. In the work of "reinventing" the church, begin the task where you are. Begin with the official leadership. If leaders reject the challenge, look for receptive persons in the congregation. If none in the congregation can share the vision, invite unchurched persons to become part of a discipleship group. (Missionaries have never had the luxury of beginning with believers, and if the church has no interest in changing for the future, you stand in a serious missionary situation.) Be steadfast in your vision and constant in your efforts.

2. Leaders! Be clear about your aim: to become an

authentic expression of the Body of Christ and to equip leaders who will help multiply active missional groups for ministries of compassion and justice.

3. Seek the guidance of the Holy Spirit to identify leaders.

4. Aim to involve the whole church in mission groups. Do not become discouraged when some strong and dependable leaders choose not to participate. Fifty or sixty percent is a good ratio.

5. Expect to invest at least five years in calling forth ministry groups with mature leadership. It may be necessary to make several starts to achieve this goal. (Note Stan Ott's experience in the opening interview.)

6. Provide experiences for your leaders to encounter other vital persons and congregations. Visit churches engaged in the process of transformation. Learn from them. Take church members to conferences, plan regular retreats, and encourage awakened persons to participate in training events both inside and beyond your own congregation. These experiences will enrich and deepen the vision of your members.

7. Do not be surprised when tension develops between the new group and the old, established leadership. Avoid being labeled "holier than thou." Be diligent in keeping communication open and suspicion to a minimum. Be patient! Significant and lasting changes require time and persistence.

8. Keep alive in the mission groups the essential elements of the church: worship, sharing, prayer, scripture, care, discernment, and outreach. Fight against the tendency to become inward looking, closed to new persons, and insensitive to the working of the Holy Spirit.

9. Keep a sharp focus on the ultimate goal: the reformation of the congregation through multiple mission groups and the worship of God in new and exciting ways that liberate lay persons for ministry. Expect one day for

the mission of the church to be carried out through mission groups led by lay pastors.

The calendar below provides a model for churches seeking to enter a New Day with maximum effectiveness.

A CALENDAR FOR THE TRANSITIONAL CONGREGATION

First Year. This year will witness the beginning of transformation efforts. Set forth an agenda for each month. After nine months leadership should revise the calendar and set the agenda for the next year. Keep ahead by at least one year.

First month. The pastor and selected leaders will review the text and decide how to present the material to the official leadership. This study may be done over four weeks or the officers may choose to schedule an overnight retreat.

Second month. Study of this text.

Third month. Introducing the text's content to the congregation. This presentation to the congregation may come via:

    — sermons

    — reading and discussing the text

    — reports from leaders

    — printing excerpts from the text in the newsletter.

Fourth month. Home meetings in the congregation, led by officers, to receive feedback on the sermons, readings, and visions of revitalization in the congregation.

Fifth month. Begin a prayer emphasis in the congregation that includes sermons and a study group that will seriously engage in the ministry of prayer. See Chapter 6 for suggestions.

Sixth month. Begin mission groups. These groups may grow out of the officers' study of the text, the prayer study group, or the interest of members in the congregation. Continue the prayer emphasis. (See Chapter 7.)

Seventh month. Keep the importance of prayer before the congregation by short testimonies in "a minute for renewal," in sermons, and in reports of answers to prayer.

Eighth month. Continue the growth of persons via mission groups and the prayer emphasis.

Ninth month. Evaluate growth of leadership in the mission group(s). Consider beginning new groups.

Tenth month. Ask the worship committee to evaluate the worship service. Spend at least three months planning ways to make worship more relevant to new persons.

Eleventh month. Evaluate the health of mission groups. The principles set forth in Chapter 7 will provide criteria for the evaluation.

Twelfth month. Plan a festival to celebrate the pain and the progress of your renewal efforts. This celebration should include reports from mission groups. Make this an exposure event by inviting persons who are not in a small group. See the interview with Richard Meyer in Chapter 7 and note the Day of Renewal.

Second Year. Focus on multiplying the number of groups in the congregation and keeping them healthy. Healthy groups worship, fellowship, reach out to new persons, and engage in mission. Help groups to discern their mission, God's call to them.

Continue the revitalization of worship.

Provide regular meetings for the nurture and direction of the lay pastors of mission groups.

Third Year. Continue to develop mission groups and enrich the worship-celebration. Invite leaders and church officials to explore how the mission of the church can be accomplished through mission groups. This shift will mean that persons do the work of ministry out of a sense of call. Such a shift from management strategy to vocational strategy proves critical for a healthy church.

Fourth Year. Increase the number of mission groups. Expand the time and form of the worship service. You may need to add an alternative worship service to accommodate the number and diversity of persons.

In this year the crucial issue will be envisioning the governance of the church. How will mission groups have their discernment affirmed by the officers? What role do officers play in the new configuration? How will officers function as spiritual leaders for the mission, the worship, and the members of the congregation?[7]

Fifth Year. Expect to have made major progress in the transformation of the church. This year should be marked with a mature vision of mission and outreach, a refinement of worship, and the work of the church increasingly accomplished through groups that worship, care, discern, and serve.

This calendar of events offers one way of approaching the task of congregational transformation. Leaders should use it as a beginning point and adapt it to their peculiar situation.

It is essential that leaders working in the transitional church keep their goals in mind. Every church has its own context, unique personality, and particular form of faithfulness. Obstacles, detours, and set-backs will occur, but the church with a clear vision will find ways to navigate the turbulent stream.

CHAPTER 6

How to Invite the Church to Pray

A friend showed me a copy of your booklet on prayer. The challenge to a 30-day experiment intrigued me, and I invited a friend in my church to engage in it with me.

Our experience convinced us that we needed a deeper spirit of prayer in our congregation so I invited ten women for lunch and explained the experiment to them. Eight accepted the challenge, and each was assigned a prayer partner. I asked them to read the suggestions in the booklet, pray each day, and keep a journal.

I met with each person weekly for the four weeks to answer questions, discuss problems, and alleviate concerns. Halfway through the experiment the group met to share their experiences. At the end of the month we had a celebration to share the joys and strengths we had experienced, as well as the problems we had dealt with. At the gathering they said things like: "I am at peace with myself and have a more joyful, thankful heart." Another said, "The prayer experience opened up the 'life line' to Christ who has always been available to me, though I didn't know it." Finally, "My prayer has become so much deeper and more meaningful."

These eight women agreed to lead eight other groups of six persons each. The same changes took place in these persons. As a result of this prayer emphasis our church has added new members, developed a prayer network, created a study group on prayer, and engaged all our lead-

ers in the prayer experiment. People around town are asking, "What is going on at First Church?"

Every one of the participants in the original group has become an elder, deacon, or officer in the church. One began Habitat for Humanity [in the community]. Our whole congregation and the entire community have felt the impact of this prayer emphasis through our meager efforts to learn to pray. Needless to say, we are excited about continuing this endless adventure! (FROM A LETTER TO BEN JOHNSON IN RESPONSE TO *AN ADVENTURE IN PRAYER*)

Prayer opens a congregation to a deeper sense of the presence of God; prayer also empowers a congregation to move with confidence from a transitional church to Future Church. This immersion in prayer may take many forms; the one reported to me in personal correspondence provides only one model. Multiple concrete options exist to create a community of prayer.

INTRODUCING A PRAYER EMPHASIS

The following should be taken as illustrative of the numerous ways to introduce a churchwide emphasis on prayer. One person who feels called to lead the church into a vital discipline of prayer provides a greater impetus to pray than any strategy one can conceive. Pray for guidance in finding such a person; invite this person to give leadership to the congregation.

The pastor fills a key role in calling the church to prayer. A series of sermons can clarify this call and challenge persons to pray. Also, the pastor's personal example, lifestyle, and passion for prayer contribute significantly.

Inform the congregation through preaching but also through articles in the church's newsletter. These articles state the need for prayer and the church's intention to seek the will of God for its life and ministry as a praying community. Personal testimonies in the newsletter add strength to the emphasis on prayer.

A "pastoral letter" to the congregation expressing the pastor's eagerness for the congregation to pray for renewal may be more effective than a newsletter article. A pastor who daily spends serious time in prayer can make clear to the membership the urgency of turning to God for new life and vision.

The following statements convey the spirit of this concern for prayer. You are free to use them without credit or permission.

☀ *Christ was central to the life and ministry of the early church. He was their life. Because of their sense of the immediate presence of the risen Lord, they prayed with confidence and carried out their mission with power.*

☀ *When we have received the gift of presence, a new measure of confidence will come to us. The transition from old structures of the church to new and relevant ones may be accompanied with anxiety; but in the certainty that Christ is with us, that he is guiding us, we can move forward. Prayer provides the context for new life and new visions; it is the place to begin our quest for the new reformation. God seems to be summoning the church to pray.*

☀ *The people of God do not need better organization as much as they need better prayer; they do not need more programs as much as they need more constant prayer; they do not need skills, techniques, or strategies as much as they need a new resolve to pray. Prayer is the greatest resource of the church searching for vitality.*

☀ *What is prayer? The soul's approach to the divine. Our proper posture before God. An encounter with the Holy. Prayer is listening for God. True prayer constitutes the soul of religion, the heart of the church, and the essence of the Christian life. Believing prayer enlivens the hearts of Christians, shapes the ministry of the church, and influences the destiny of the world. What could be more important to a struggling, declining church than recovering the art of prayer?*

* *In these transitional years we are calling the church to prayer with the hope that we will become more aware of God's presence, be filled with a new measure of hope and confidence, and experience the liberation of our creative imaginations. If the presence of Christ permeates the consciousness of the church, we will move into the future with assurance and hope.*

* *Prayer not only puts us in the place to receive the presence of God and to find new security, it also opens us to the creative power of God. Guidance most often comes to God's people when they pray. Recall Peter in Joppa (Acts 10), Paul in Antioch (Acts 13), and the persecuted church in Jerusalem (Acts 8). Prayer led each of these groups of disciples into the deep movement of the Holy Spirit who inspired in them intuitions and imaginations of the future. Expect the future church to emerge from deep prayer experiences rather than conferences on goal setting.*

* *A church that recovers both its corporate and personal life of prayer positions itself to hear God speak a saving and redemptive word; a church that has been called can speak with confidence; a church that has been sent can go with assurance; and a church that has spent time in the divine presence can influence the places of its ministry.*

Invite Specific Commitments to Prayer

After informing the church of the importance and timeliness of prayer, invite members to make a prayer commitment. The intentional commitment of persons to pray marks the beginning of their prayer life.

Offer interested persons guidance in prayer. A number of persons may be interested in participating in the prayer ministry of the church but lack knowledge and skills in the practice of prayer. Offer them a basic seminar on prayer.[1]

Most beginners in prayer confess two problems: how to begin and how to keep at the task. If persons in your church have these concerns, share with them the following "helps" as a bulletin insert.

To Pray Effectively

1. Begin where you are in the art of prayer. Actually, you can't begin anywhere else. Acknowledge your desire for God. Locate inside yourself the yearning for God.

Through the centuries, prayer, in all its forms, has helped serious persons deepen their desire for God.

2. Obey what the Spirit of God says to you. The Holy Spirit has myriad ways to reveal God to us — scripture, preaching, the church's memory, the witness of a friend, and the action of the Spirit to name a few. God's revelation comes in the form of a word or words, in images, intuitions, imaginations, and the providence of our lives.

However God's will is made known, obey it. Disobedience blunts the sense of the Spirit's presence and dulls our desire for God. When we fail in our obedience, we must confess our sin and begin anew without either berating ourselves or making excuses. Beginning a life of obedience is not a mysterious act, as Englishman George MacDonald makes quite clear:

But you can be a disciple of the Living One — by obeying him in the first thing you can think of in which you are not now obeying him. We must learn to obey him in everything, and so must begin somewhere. Let it be at once and in the very next thing that lies at the door of our conscience.[2]

3. Discern with others the call of God. Prayer postures us to hear the Lord speak. Listen for a personal word and a word for the church of Jesus Christ. The Spirit gives discernment of both.

Danger may lurk along this narrow road of vision and revelation, but times like ours demand high levels of risk. Old ways have proven ineffective and the new ways are waiting to be born. Congregations with confidence in the risen Lord and his word, must lead the way through this transitional era. As the Lord of the church speaks, each congregation must discern its role in the reconstruction of the church.

INTRODUCE NEW FORMS OF PRAYER

The basic suggestions we have made need to be enlarged when the congregation takes seriously the call to prayer. In weekly classes, workshops, or sermons, the congregation should be instructed in challenging ways to pray. These basic forms of prayer may include corporate, personal, life-centered, bonding, and contemplative prayer. Decide on the best way to introduce these forms of prayer. Consider the following:

1. Provide instruction in these five forms of prayer in a series of sermons. If you choose this option provide the congregation a bulletin insert that outlines the prayer form being presented on a particular Sunday.

2. Invite interested members to explore these five ways of prayer as a group. Offer them a seminar that

includes instruction, experience, and accountability. See Appendix A for guidance in conducting the seminar.

3. If the whole congregation cannot embrace this emphasis, begin with a group of six or eight persons.

CORPORATE PRAYER

The worship of God is the corporate prayer of the church. The order of worship contains precisely those elements that mark mature prayer — praise, confession, intercession, listening, and offering ourselves to God. When persons engage in worship without being conscious of their encounter with God, no dialogue occurs. As a way of strengthening your church's sense of the presence of God, teach them to "worship in awareness," that is, focus on each movement in worship as a means of communion with God. Doing so will deepen sensitivity to God's presence. Remind the congregation to participate in the liturgy as a corporate prayer:

PRELUDE. A time to quiet your mind, turn your thoughts from the week's activities to God. In these quiet moments become focused on the presence of God.

CALL TO WORSHIP. Listen for God's Spirit calling you into the divine presence. Give your loving consent to come and "appear before God."

> "Enter into his gates with thanksgiving and into his courts with praise!"

HYMN OF PRAISE. Be aware that you are in the presence of the Most Holy God. Let your praise and adoration arise with that of the whole community to bring honor to God.

> "Praise God from whom all blessings flow."

PRAYER OF CONFESSION. The holiness of God makes us aware of our sinfulness and calls us to confess our sin. Read the prayer of confession; think about specific sins in your life and the life of the church. Put your heart in the words of confession. Listen for and celebrate the forgiveness of sins in Jesus Christ.

"In Christ we are forgiven!"

SCRIPTURE READINGS. Prepare to hear the Lord speak to you through these ancient texts. For centuries God has been made known through the text of Holy Scripture and is still revealed there today.

"Listen for God."

PROCLAMATION. The minister of God seeks to speak for God, to interpret the text as God's word to us today. Listen to the words of the minister but listen beyond the human words for the Word of God.

"Speak Lord, your servant hears."

PRAYERS OF THE PEOPLE. Follow the words of the liturgist. Pray them in your mind. These prayers express the intercessions and petitions of the people of God.

"Lord, hear our prayer."

OFFERING. Place your offering in the collection plate to symbolize the dedication of your life to God. Worship calls forth such dedication.

"Take my life and let it be consecrated Lord to thee."

BENEDICTION. Receive the blessing of God upon your life for the ensuing week. (You may wish to write out the benediction so you can use it in your personal prayer and thereby extend the blessing received on the Lord's Day throughout the week.) Go forth in the confidence that your life has been united to the one who created and governs the world. Live confidently that God's will will be done on earth as in heaven.

"The grace of the Lord Jesus Christ is with me."

As persons make each service of worship a corporate prayer their lives will be transformed through the Spirit.

PERSONAL PRAYER

The corporate prayer of the church provides the form for our personal prayer. Our prayers are personal but not private because we always pray as a member of Christ's body and we are always praying with Christ who ever lives to make intercession for us.

While the corporate prayer of the church provides the form of our prayer, liturgical prayer alone does not prove sufficient for our daily needs. Because of the distractions of the world and the waywardness of our own hearts, we must come before God daily with our needs and desires and gratitude. This daily meeting with God deepens our consciousness of the divine presence, purifies our hearts, and gives us strength to live in obedience.

If the characteristic need of corporate prayer is awareness, personal prayer requires intentionality. Most agree on the value and necessity of prayer, but many of us find disciplined regularity in prayer difficult.

Regular prayer becomes easier when persons have a good pattern to follow. The liturgy of the Lord's Day offers a good model. Personal prayer and corporate prayer follow the same order and mutually reinforce each other.

Growth in personal prayer requires a conscientious commitment to a time and place for prayer. The following suggestions may help persons expand the corporate prayer of worship in their daily exercise of prayer:

PRELUDE. The prelude to personal prayer consists of relaxation, spiritual reading, and meditation. Begin your time of prayer by getting seated comfortably and relaxing your body. You will be better able to focus on God if you release the tensions in your body.

READ THE SCRIPTURES. The Psalms have long been the prayer book of our faith. Read a Psalm each day.

In addition, read a selection from a Gospel or an Epistle. Turn your attention to God. Think about the greatness and majesty of God. Wonder at the fact that God knows you and loves you. Let your soul be lost in awe before the Lord your Maker.

PRAISE. From your meditation let your heart praise God. A hymn of praise will provide you with words. No need to name everything for which you can praise God; one thing each day will suffice.

CONFESS. Recall the past twenty-four hours of your life. Confess the sins of which you are aware— sins of thought, word, and deed. Believe that God is more eager to forgive your sins than you are to acknowledge them.

PETITION AND INTERCESSION. Bring to God the deepest desires of your heart. Speak them simply to one who loves you like a Parent, who listens to your every utterance, and desires the fulfillment of your life.

You will not know the changes accomplished by prayer until history has ended and God shows us what human prayer achieved. Pray about the least of issues as well as the greatest.

OFFERING. Offer yourself to God for this day. Renew the vows that you made when you were baptized, confirmed, or ordained. "Not my will but thine be done" is the prayer of perfect surrender.

SILENCE. Spend a few minutes in silence. Wait for the Lord to speak. Do not be alarmed if no thoughts come to your mind. Keep listening for God throughout the day.

BENEDICTION. Since we cannot give ourselves a blessing, remember the benediction which was given to you at the close of worship on the Lord's Day. Repeat the benediction to extend it into the entire week.

LIFE-CENTERED PRAYER

God, the Creator and Sustainer of the world, has not vacated the cosmos, but continues to unfold a divine purpose in human history. God is at work in everything!

God does not purpose everything, but is in everything for good. Because God is in everything, every event in life provides us an opportunity to respond to God. To be aware of God, to welcome God in these events, leads into a living communion with the divine mystery. Many persons growing in prayer have found these suggestions helpful:

Gather the Day

Think back over the day and identify the major movements in it. The paragraphs of the day might include morning prayer, dressing for the day, trip to work, an appointment, a telephone call, a new opportunity, a trip to the doctor, etc. List these movements of your day.

Review the Day

Read over the list of events. Make no judgments, do not shun painful memories, avoid excuses for yourself. These events form the substance of your life; this is the person God loves; this is the person in whom God is working out a purpose.

Give Thanks for the Day

Think back over your day, visualize each of the occurrences, and give thanks to God for your life and the happenings of the day.

Make Confession of Sin

As you review your life confess the thoughts, words, or deeds in which you have sinned against God, your neighbor, or yourself.

Wonder at the Meaning of the Events

As you think about each of the movements in your life ask questions like these:

☀ What was God saying to me in this event?

- ☀ What am I being called to do?
- ☀ How does this event connect with the rest of my life?
- ☀ What hints about the future did this day hold?

BONDING PRAYER

Scripture urges us to "pray for one another" (James 5:16). Different visions of God's will for the church can produce tensions that strain our unity to the breaking point. Prayer unites, reconciles, and bonds us together. Let us call the church to pray for one another.

Amazing changes occur when we pray for another member of the Body of Christ. You cannot hate a person for whom you pray regularly. Prayer narrows the distance between us. Prayer gives birth to generous attitudes and sympathetic feelings. Caring prayer creates community.

For whom do we pray?

1. Family. Pray for the immediate members of your family. Remember those who seek to be faithful and need encouragement. Pray for the indulgent and rebellious. Pray especially for the sick and the troubled. And, give thanks for family blessings.

2. Friends. Remember friends who have faithfully supported you throughout your life. Remember those also who depend on you for love, care, and affirmation.

3. Enemies. "But I say to you, love your enemies and pray for those who persecute you" (Matt. 5:44). "Enemy" may be too strong a term. Try praying for your antagonists, for those who irritate, offend, hurt, or discount you.

4. Partners. Many congregations have been greatly strengthened by a prayer partner program. Members of the congregation choose a person for whom they pray daily. Begin such a movement in your congregation.

5. Groups. Every group in the church deserves our prayer: committees, choirs, teachers, task forces, church officers. Pray by name for every person in these various

groups. Meetings will progress more smoothly and show greater creativity, tasks will be accomplished more easily, and relationships will deepen because we have prayed for those involved.

6. Marginal members. About half the members of every church can be classified as marginal. Distribute the names of marginal members to an intercessory prayer group. Saturate lonely, alienated persons with faithful, believing prayer!

7. Leadership. Pray for those persons who are in spiritual leadership. The Apostle Paul admonished Timothy, "I urge that supplications, prayers, intercessions, and thanksgivings be made for everyone, for kings and all who are in high positions" (1 Tim. 2:1-2). Pastors, elders, and committee chairs all need our prayers, as well as governors, senators, and presidents. Leaders are empowered when we pray for them.

Here are four ways to pray for others:

1. Your Words. Put into words the deepest desires of your heart for another person. Ask for that person's health, an increase of knowledge, clarity in discernment of God's will, and strength to obey.

2. God's Word. If you lack words of your own, pray the text of scripture. For example:

> And this is my prayer, that your love may overflow more and more with knowledge and full insight to help you to determine what is best, so that in the day of Christ you may be pure and blameless, having produced the harvest of righteousness that comes through Jesus Christ for the glory and praise of God (Phil. 1:9-11).

Pray a Psalm and insert the name of the person for whom you are praying. For example:

> O, Lord, you have searched____and known____. You know when____ sits down and when ____ rises up; you discern ____'s thoughts from afar. Search____, O God, and know____'s heart! Try

and know_____'s thoughts! And see if there is any wicked way in_____, and lead _____ in the way everlasting (Psalm 139: 1-2, 23-24).

3. Spontaneous Words. Offer prayers throughout the day. For example: in a group meeting, a choir rehearsal, at a fellowship dinner, we can pray for persons without ceasing the conversation or changing the expression on our face. Spontaneous prayers like "bless you," "God loves you," or "God help you," make it easy to pray for another without closing our eyes or moving our lips.

4. Creative Images. Persons who have difficulty praying in words find that they can pray in images or pictures. Imagine Christ with the person for whom you are praying. Visualize him receiving, touching, healing, and making this person whole. Words are unnecessary. The picture is the prayer.

QUIET PRAYER

Quiet prayer may be the most creative form of prayer for re-visioning the transitional church. In the silence God comes to us, claims us, and communicates to us at a depth beyond our actions, feelings, and thinking. From this silence come intuitions and imaginations that can shape Future Church.

This form of prayer has a long and rich tradition. It goes by various names: centering prayer, the prayer of quiet, or contemplative prayer. Quiet prayer refers to a kind of prayer in which requests diminish, words fall away, feelings no longer have importance, and our hearts wait in silence before God.

The "prayer of silence" permits our personal and collective consciousness to open up to the creative presence of God. From this depth comes divine guidance for our individual and corporate life. Often the communication comes to us in images and intuitions.

A few tested practices may help us to enter the silence:

1. Find a quiet place.

2. Get seated comfortably; sit erect.

3. Take deep breaths, inhaling and exhaling slowly, relaxing with each breath.

4. Repeat the text: "Be still and know that I am God." Begin to recite the text in rhythm with your breathing.

5. Gradually slow the repetition of the text until the words drop away altogether and your mind focuses on the center, and your attention settles on God.

6. When distracting thoughts arise, notice them, but withhold your interest. Gently return to the center.

7. Spend fifteen or twenty minutes giving God your loving attention. You may begin with only three or four minutes, but increase your time as you become comfortable with the silence. Don't fret. Don't work at it. Let things be.

8. At the end of your silence, pay attention to the ideas that come to you through images, symbols, or dreams. God has new and creative ideas for the church and when we learn to be quiet and open, God will show them to us.

LISTEN TO GOD TOGETHER

For the church to be reshaped by prayer, the architects of the congregation and the denomination will benefit from efforts to enter the silence together and listen for the Word of God. Many churches of the Reformation have become so "word" oriented that they commonly assume God acts only as someone is speaking. Perhaps the Quakers have learned a lesson about silence that could be instructive for many of us.

For a group committed to spending time together listening for God these suggestions may be of benefit:

1. Begin each officers' meeting with a half hour of silence. In the silence, listen to God for guidance for the congregation.

If you cannot begin with a half hour, try a few minutes and increase the time. In the silence, today's church can receive the illumination of the Spirit and the energy that comes from an encounter with Christ.

2. Encourage committees to begin each meeting with a period of silence in which they focus on God and seek guidance for their task.

3. Encourage individuals to listen to God for guidance in their personal lives. Provide a way for them to share with the pastor and leaders their inspirations.

Emphasis on these forms of prayer over a period of time will transform the life of the congregation. As new life breaks forth, look for ways to nurture it and direct it toward the renewal of the whole congregation.

Imagine the quality of worship, fellowship, and mission when a congregation grounds its life in prayer!

THE VISION

When a congregation turns toward God in prayer, it will find a surprising response from the Holy One. As members begin to center their attention upon God, all the issues facing the church appear in a new light. People who pray together find a depth of unity and love unreachable by human striving.

This environment of prayer provides the pre-condition for a vision of the future. Believing communities open to the Spirit of God will be the pace-setters for Future Church. Like the Spirit moving upon the Valley of Dry Bones, God will move upon our churches, fill them with life and raise them up to serve the divine purpose.

CHAPTER 7

How to Create Dynamic Mission Groups

Two years ago I came to a traditional church with no history of small groups. To begin establishing small groups I preached several sermons on Jesus and the twelve, pointing to his approach to nurturing and training his followers. In one of the sermons I suggested that in a year or two we wanted to have groups like that in our church. Then on an officers' retreat we used Jesus' model of small group sharing to permit our leaders to participate in a small group.

After a few months in the parish I invited ten persons to join me in a small group experience, first for their own growth and second so that they could eventually become leaders of new groups. We met together for nine months sharing our faith, praying, reading scripture, and working through a book I had written, **One Anothering**. By the time we finished the book these group participants were ready to begin leading new groups.

To facilitate the formation of new groups we planned a Day of Renewal. We invited everyone in the congregation to attend and the program consisted of members of the original small group telling about their discoveries. Instruction was given for participating in a group and an opportunity was offered for new persons to sign up. From that day came six new groups. We began anticipating the formation of other groups as leaders developed.

When I am asked, "Why do you believe in the small group as a way of 'being the church'?" I *explain that it is a biblical model, responsive to people's need for support and growth, a way of doing ministry with the whole people of God, and, frankly, I find enormous support for my own life and ministry.*

I look forward to the day when the ministry of our whole congregation will have a small group base. Healthy groups engage in all the functions of the church — worship, fellowship, service, and outreach. And, when the mission arises from the small group, all the members are learning to be the church. (INTERVIEW WITH RICHARD MEYER, PASTOR, MAITLAND PRESBYTERIAN CHURCH IN MAITLAND, FL.)

In our proposal for the transitional church we have suggested that every congregation needs a core group of dedicated disciples. We believe these groups offer one highly effective way to recover a sense of the presence of God, liberate the laity, and shift the church's posture from maintenance to mission. The kind of groups we advocate will seek the presence of God in praise and worship; they will provide a core group of dedicated disciples; they will generate the desire for transformation in worship; they will provide a setting in which lay persons may learn ways of effective ministry by discerning God's call, showing compassion in response to human pain, and learning to notice the presence of God at work in the world. These groups will become communities of discernment and active participants in mission.

The formation of apostolic groups cannot be achieved by making "small groups" one more program of the church. These groups, I believe, must become the new way the transitional church structures its life and performs its ministry. For several decades, various types of small groups have been formed in congregations — prayer groups, growth groups, self-help groups, 12-step groups, meditation groups, study groups. These special purpose groups perform worthy functions in the congregation, but we are calling for something quite different. We are urging the creation of full-service groups that carry out the mission of the congregation. This model suggests a shift from small groups with special purposes (which often become focused only on their own members), to groups that mature into communities of worship, fellowship, nurture, and mission.

How do these mission groups differ from other small groups? Obviously they share many practices and aims with other small groups, but these mission groups are distinguished by their inclusion of all the functions of the church — worship, nurture, outreach, and mission. These groups, in contrast with fellowship groups, seek to expand their life by constantly adding new persons. These are not "closed" groups. Other types of groups have a leader, but these groups will be pastored by a lay pastor. The lay pastor, approved by the governing body, becomes accountable to this body for the life and ministry of the mission group. Because the church's mission will eventually be conducted through mission groups, their formation and growth must have the approval of the governing body.

THE BIBLICAL FOUNDATION FOR MISSION GROUPS

The model set forth in Jesus' own ministry offers sufficient reason for the formation of mission groups, and Jesus' work with the disciples provides a pattern worthy of imitation. The disciples followed the example of Jesus in forming mission groups (Acts 2:42-47 and 13:1-3) and many believe that this strategy fueled the expansion of the early church. The emphases Jesus used with his disciple-band can guide us in the formation of effective mission groups. Perhaps this is the reason that Gareth W. Icenogle uses Jesus and the twelve as a way of introducing his foundation for small groups.[1]

1. Jesus was himself the center of the group. He

called the group together around himself and provided their nurture. "The twelve looked to Jesus as their director, model, teacher, brother and friend."[2] All Christian groups since this original one have looked to Jesus as the founding person and controlling influence. He, therefore, must stand at the center of mission groups.

2. The first group was created out of a heterogeneous culture. Among the followers of Jesus were fishermen, tax collectors, and revolutionaries, yet Jesus was able to mold these diverse persons into a unified community of love. Groups built on this foundation will provide a safe approach for mainline churches to break out of their homogeneous culture. Different kinds of persons can be more easily integrated into a small group than a large one. Persons from different cultures, when joined together in a small group, build relational bridges into the larger congregation. The missional group offers the best prospect for congregations to become diverse and inclusive.

3. Mission propelled the life and activity of the group. From the outset, those who clustered around Jesus knew that they were engaging in a mission. "Follow me and I will make you fish for people" (Matt. 4:19). To follow him meant participating in his mission. Like modern disciples, Peter and John struggled with personal gain and a place of honor, but Jesus did not allow selfishness to dominate his companions. By his teaching and example, Jesus continuously emphasized the worldly orientation of his small community of followers. Mission groups today must answer the call to join Jesus Christ in his service to the world.

4. The twelve shared life together. Persons in the band of followers shared meals, travels, tasks, and retreats together. They spoke with each other about their hopes and fears. Along with their own needs, they considered the needs of the crowd that always pressed heavily upon their close fellowship. Their life together had to be shared with the world.

5. The community of the twelve provided a model for the larger society. In creating this close, missional community, Jesus showed the selfish, greedy, alienated world the intention of God. This community of disciples demonstrated the love and forgiveness he taught the multitudes. Following the emphasis of Jesus, Paul knew that the life of his congregations validated his verbal message. Demonstrations of faith, hope, love, and sacrifice authenticated the message. By the same token disunity and sin called into question the message.

6. Jesus and the twelve offered a model of life that contradicted the culture. In Jesus' day the culture valued the display of wealth, gaining honor from others, and shaming those who were poor and marginalized. Jesus and the twelve practiced renunciation, humility, and love. Their unselfish practices called into question the dominant cultural values. In today's world of greed, competition, and individualism, mission groups built on this model will provide diversity, inclusivity, and unity. These communities of faith will also challenge the church's culture as well as the society at large.

7. This group of twelve disciples experienced the reality of the eternal family. Despite differences in their backgrounds and personalities, Christ united his followers as brothers in one household. Their life centered in Jesus Christ; they called God, "Father," and recognized Jesus as brother; they sought to carry out the will of God in the world. The relationships and commitments experienced in small groups often become deeper and more committed than even family relationships.

8. Jesus' small group demonstrated a new power structure. Previously power was experienced as force guaranteed by swords, spears, and armies. The disciples, following the example of Jesus, unleashed a new kind of power characterized by love, sacrifice, and suffering. Their capacity to care for broken, marginalized persons wielded a power greater than the sword of Caesar. Their willingness to risk death for the sake of Christ marked a

new level of commitment. By the power of love and sacrifice, this valiant body of believers toppled the Roman Empire. What would this kind of power mean in our world?

9. Jesus' community was both broken and resurrected. In the arrest, trial, and crucifixion of Jesus, his followers experienced broken relationships, dreams, and hopes. The tragic events at the close of Jesus' life shattered the disciples' image of the future. But the resurrection restored their confidence. The resurrection and the gift of the Spirit gave the disciples a sense of Jesus' presence with them, even in them. With this awareness of his presence they envisioned continuing the work he had begun. Through the intervening years the alternating experience of brokenness and resurrection has remained constant with the followers of Christ.

If the church expects to receive new life through these mission groups, it must build them on the kind of foundation laid by Jesus in his own ministry. The principles Jesus used in forming the twelve provide a rich source for imagining the nature, structure, and life of modern groups.

CLARIFY GOALS FOR MISSION GROUPS

Without clearly defined goals, mission groups will lose focus and turn inward. Building mature groups will be aided greatly by a statement of purpose. Goals also provide a basis for evaluation and correction. Consider these ten goals for mission groups as a starter for your own goals:

1. Missions groups will worship and glorify God. God stands at the center of all our efforts. Creation, Redemption, and Kingdom — all exist for God's greater glory. Therefore, the worship of God must stand at the center of the group's life. Through scripture, prayer, song, and praise, God is worshipped and glorified.

2. Mission groups will provide centers of life and transformation for individuals and for the congregation. Akin to those early communities of faith, these groups will gather around Jesus Christ. "Where two or three are gathered, I am in their midst." The worship of Christ and the sharing of life together in love offers a transformative energy in the congregation. These vital centers offer a place for new persons to connect, for marginal persons to be formed, and for new visions of the church to be born.

3. Mission groups will train persons in discipleship. In this trusting fellowship persons learn to pray, to speak of their deepest needs, to witness to their experience of Christ, and to find help with personal failure. By providing a nurturing environment, the group becomes a school of Christian living. In addition to the basic disciplines of the Christian life, group members learn discernment as they work out the call of God; they learn ministry by participating in the mission of the group.

4. Mission groups will reach new persons. Christ's mission to the world has always been two-fold: conversion and service. Without the conversion of new persons the mission dies; without sacrificial service to others the mission is betrayed. Because of this evangelistic imperative for the church, members of mission groups have both an evangelistic mission and a ministry of compassion. The mission group reaches out to new persons through relationships, and new persons experience the faith by participating in the group. If the mission group does not grow, it will die.

5. Mission groups will offer care to each of the members. Caring for persons in pain rested at the heart of Jesus' ministry. Expressive of this same Spirit, members of the group care for each other by listening to joys and sorrows, by being with each other in times of stress, by offering a helping hand at the time of need. Christians have always distinguished themselves by the way they "love one another."

6. Mission groups will welcome diversity. Just as Jesus' followers covered a broad spectrum of social, economic, and political life, these groups will unite culturally diverse persons. This unity can only occur as the group keeps its focus on Jesus Christ; the Spirit of Jesus has the power to unite diverse people because he stands within and above every culture. To discover this unity, the group will need to provide a "safe place" for different kinds of persons to speak and interact honestly. Whether the difference is racial, political, cultural, or sexual, the safety of the group permits all members to experience the redemptive, transformative power of Jesus Christ.

7. Mission groups will discover a ministry. Jesus' call to follow him into the world provides the impetus for ministry. In the world we join Jesus in service to the poor, the broken, the marginalized, and the powerless. To engage in effective ministry the group will discern its context: Where is the pain in our community? Where does oppression occur? Whose voice is not being heard? These questions will both uncover hurt and help groups identify their particular mission.

8. Mission groups will develop lay pastors. Not only does the group train persons for discipleship, but it also provides a "school" for developing new leaders. All groups begin with a lay leader and an associate. By observing the role of the leader and by assisting in the leadership, the associate learns to lead. Eventually, the associate leader becomes the leader of the group or begins a new one. Every mission group has the task of discerning the gift of leadership in its members. As group members discern gifts, they point them out to other members and nurture them. This important work can best be done as members regularly experience the gifts of other members.

9. Mission groups will multiply. The number of groups must multiply until the life of the congregation has been permeated with a new spirit and has been restructured to express its mission through these apostolic groups. Eventually, the entire mission of the church will

be carried out through mission groups. For this vision to materialize, groups must multiply and the church's structure must flex.

Groups multiply by dividing existing groups, by beginning new groups with visitors or new members; groups multiply intentionally by starting special purpose groups for divorced persons, for new parents, or for the unemployed, to cite a few examples.

10. Mission groups will revitalize the congregation and call forth a new way of being the church. The groups center their life in Christ and seek to bring glory and praise to God through worship. The scriptures (perhaps the lectionary passages) provide the substance of their worship and their experience of the text is brought into the celebration; members who have been renewed through their group participation enrich corporate worship. The faith and hope born in these fellowships begin to pervade the life of the congregation. As persons become serious disciples, their life and influence add leaven to the congregation.

As you form groups in the congregation, consider these suggestions as a starting place for stating your particular goals. Adjust, modify, or add to these goals until you have established clear goals for your mission groups. Begin the first groups and regularly evaluate their progress by your clearly defined goals. Both the foundation set forth in Jesus' relationship with the twelve and these goals should be shared with members in all your groups.

DEVELOP LAY LEADERSHIP

Effective mission groups require strong leadership. Since the foundation for defining Future Church in part depends upon the vitality of mission groups, it proves essential to develop a plan for selecting, equipping, and supporting lay leaders.

Mission groups should be led by lay persons who have felt a call to this ministry. The first leader may be the ordained minister who calls together the first group of disciples. From this group can be drawn leaders for new groups. As groups multiply and mature, members should identify additional leaders. The interview with Richard Meyer clearly illustrates each of these points.

Use the apprentice method to develop new leaders. In the first group, the pastor will select a lay associate. The associate leader learns by participating in the group; by observing the pastor, the associate learns the format, aims, and goals of leadership. Eventually, he or she shares in leading the group. This hands-on style of training develops effective leadership. Each group should always have a leader and an associate in training.

The style of the leader will be that of a player/coach, not that of a drill sergeant. The player/coach plays the game to the fullest but carries an added sense of responsibility for the team. The coach points out new directions, analyzes behavior, and sorts out relational problems. This participant/observer role of leaders requires careful attention to the dynamics of the group while participating in those dynamics.

To be effective, lay leaders require ongoing support by the pastor. Imagine that you have four mission groups led by four lay pastors and their associates-in-training. How will these leaders get the support, training, and care they need to effectively pastor these groups?

The need for equipping requires the ordained minister to become a "pastor to the pastors." These lay leaders of mission groups meet every other week with the minister for guidance, support, and continuous training. This meeting must not become a business meeting for reports and accounting (the old Constantinian way), but a modeling of the new way of ministry. For example, the lay leaders' meeting will begin with prayer; they will read scripture together to listen for the voice of God; they will spend time in silence discerning God's guidance.

Out of their listening to the Word and from their silence, lay pastors will share what they are hearing. They will talk about problems and issues facing their mission groups. From this continuous training the leaders gain wisdom for supporting and directing their small communities. These gatherings will also include sharing the joys of new life being born in their groups, progress in the mission, and the new persons that have become part of the fellowship since the last meeting.

In addition to the renewal and support lay pastors receive, this bi-weekly meeting provides opportunity for discernment. As mission groups consider various options for mission, this support group will provide a context for mutual discernment. Seeking corporate discernment in this training group will assist the discernment of the governing body.

This gathering of lay pastors also provides a place for the minister to present mission challenges. Mission to the wider community presents one set of opportunities for mission groups, but the need for ministry in the congregation presents another. Ministries like welcoming strangers, mentoring the youth, arranging chairs in the fellowship hall, and a host of other needs may become the calling of mission groups. As groups recognize the opportunities for ministry and feel called by God to their tasks, jobs in the church are transformed into "callings." The difference will be incredible.

BASIC GROUP FORMATION ISSUES

By reviewing the basic issues involved in establishing a new group, we aim to sponsor vital, transformative groups. With respect to the number in each group, they should be composed of ten or twelve persons who covenant to meet together, share significant disciplines, worship, and pray in order to fulfill the mission of Jesus Christ. These fellowships take seriously the call of Jesus to "come follow me."

Where will the fellowship meet? When they gather for a meeting, what order will assist them in moving toward the goals they have adopted? How often and how long will the group meet? What format will the meeting take? We will address each of these sequentially.

WHERE? The composition of the group influences the place of the meeting. Groups may meet in homes, offices, restaurants, the church, or in other, innovative settings. We encourage meeting outside the church. The office or home presents fewer barriers to new persons. The place of the meeting will in part be governed by the need for privacy and quiet. The place should also provide comfortable seating for face-to-face contact.

WHEN? What day of the week and hour of the day? Choose a time most convenient for the participants.

HOW OFTEN? The frequency may be established by the group, the pastor, or the governing body. The more frequent the meeting, the greater the care and continuity. Groups must meet at least bi-weekly; weekly will be better. Decide on weekly or bi-weekly meetings.

HOW LONG? To prescribe the length of the gathering may feel artificial, but a starting and ending time will provide security and reduce conflict. Consider meeting for 1 1/2 hours weekly or 2 hours bi-weekly. Guard the time carefully. If the group requires more time, negotiate a change.

WHAT FORMAT? The format of the meeting will vary according to the group, but each gathering should include at least four elements. In Acts, the new disciples "devoted themselves to the apostles' teaching and fellowship, to the breaking of bread and the prayers" (Acts 2:42). Their practices provide clues for life in the group.

Apostolic Teaching. Groups will base their life on the apostles' teaching—the scriptures. The Bible is the authority for faith and practice in mission groups.

Fellowship. The early church shared concerns with each other and gave each other support. So must we.

Prayer. The life of the early fellowship was grounded in prayer. Disciplined people are a praying people.

Breaking Bread. In the early church the disciples shared meals together. Each meal ended with a service of communion. While the original church broke bread together frequently, probably this practice is best reserved for the celebration of the whole community.

Silence. In addition to the four practices listed in Acts 2:42, mission groups will benefit from corporate silence. To hear God, we must learn to listen for God in silence.

An agenda for the gathering might be:

1. Gathering and greeting.

2. Call to worship—extemporaneous or using verses from scripture.

3. Singing of praise. (This works better if someone in the group plays an instrument.)

4. Reading scripture. Perhaps a Psalm plus Old and New Testament readings. (Study questions on these texts may be assigned at the previous meeting).

5. A period of silence observed after each reading.

6. Sharing out of the silence. Persons share what they have heard from God and the response they feel called to make.

7. Sharing of concerns.

8. Prayer. The sharing of concerns may be interspersed with prayer for each need. Persons benefit from hearing their names called in prayer.

9. Reports on discernment of the mission (or action in the mission since the last meeting). This space allows persons to speak about needs and opportunities. Also, intuitions may arise from the silence regarding mission.

10. Closure, prayers, notices for the next meeting.

A Second Format

An alternative format has been proposed by Dr. E. Dixon Junkin, former director of discipleship for the Presbyterian Church (U.S.A.). He proposes that the church form clusters of intentional communities that:

1. Pray together;
2. Share joys and struggles;
3. Study their context;
4. Listen for God's voice speaking through scripture;
5. Discern the obedience to which they are called;
6. Engage in common ministry.

Though stated differently, these six corporate actions also express the essence of the apostolic fellowship and provide a second way of developing group life.

Neither of these formats inhibits the creativity and initiative of the Spirit within the group. As groups continue to meet, read scripture, share, and pray, they will find their own rhythm. The best structure will grow out of the shared life of the group. Get started, be sensitive to the Spirit's guidance, and keep a balance between the inward and outward mission.

Stages in a Group's Life

Expect mission groups to pass through predictable stages. A series of rhyming words denotes predictable passages in the life of a group: born, form, storm, norm, and mourn.

1. Groups are *born*. Effective groups are born, not organized. To begin groups, sound the need, issue the invitation, and work with those who respond. The mechanical division of the parish into geographical groups will not work.

2. Groups *form*. In their formation period, groups agree to covenants that include: time, place, frequency,

format, and leadership. In the formation period, groups discuss long-range goals. Sharing life stories helps groups with their formation.

3. Groups *storm.* When the newness and fascination fade and persons become more open and honest, conflict usually arises. When the preliminary "surface unity" extends over several months, it will be tested by genuine differences of opinion. Conflict often follows. Healthy conflict leads to authentic community. Without honesty and the facing of conflicting views and feelings, a group remains superficial and will never mature into an intentional community.

4. Groups *norm.* In the context of the goals and covenants established, group members learn to live and work together in ministry. Leadership, patterns of interaction, ways of discernment, and the format for life together evolve, and life in the group runs smoothly.

5. Groups *mourn.* Groups will not remain; they will change. New persons added to the group cause change; persons leaving the group precipitate change; the division of a group to form a new group creates change and often meets resistance for that very reason; the change of leadership creates pain. All these changes in the life of a group cause grief and pain that result in members grieving the losses. Persons must recognize that grief created by change may be a modest price to pay for growth, expansion, and the multiplication of ministry.

Expecting these movements in the life-cycle of a group gives confidence that changes are normal and the assurance that changes can be productive in creating mature groups. Informed groups become better functioning groups.

THE IMPORTANCE OF EVALUATION

Regularly evaluate the life of groups to keep them on track. An evaluation pushes the group to examine its life and to reaffirm its purposes. Questions that correspond to the goals help define your progress or problems:

1. Is worship central for this group? Do we sing, pray, and worship to the glory of God?

2. Are members' lives being changed? Do new persons experience the presence of Christ in our midst?

3. What evidence do we see that persons are growing in their discipleship? Do persons pray, speak about their faith, show love and compassion, and participate in the mission?

4. Are we reaching out to new persons? Who has joined our fellowship since the last evaluation?

5. Do we provide care for each other? Who presently requires our love and support?

6. Do we welcome cultural diversity? Who represents this diversity in our group?

7. Have we discerned our mission? What options are we considering today?

8. Who within our group shows gifts for leadership? Have we spoken to the person about using these gifts?

9. Can our group divide into two groups? What effort is the congregation making to multiply groups?

10. How does our group contribute to the revitalization of the congregation? What evidence of change do we see in the congregation?

A REVIEW

The task of forming small groups for ministry and renewal must be informed by the scriptural model of Jesus. These principles, plus the goals for these groups, provide guidelines for both lay pastors and group members. Informing members about the goals, format, and the evaluation will make for healthier, more productive groups.

The driving vision for this small group formation in established mainline congregations cannot be limited to a few groups for nurture and personal growth. The transformation may begin with the pastor and one small group, but groups must multiply and mature. As these groups increasingly mirror the church in microcosm, the ministry of the congregation will be lodged in these mission groups. As these groups prayerfully discern their call, have confirmation from the governing body, and engage in ministry, the ministry of the congregation shifts from a management model to an organic, Spirit-directed model in which all involved persons have a sense of call. Lay pastors take responsibility for the health, growth, and ministry of the group under their care. This dynamic transformation in the established church will transform it into a transitional church. As the transitional church matures, it will develop structures for its life and ministry that cannot be predicted because form follows function, not the other way around. When these new forms have emerged, Future Church will become a reality.

CHAPTER 8

How to Revitalize Your Worship

If you came to our church on a Sunday morning, it would look very different from the form of worship five years ago. Some would say that the sacred space is noisy rather than quiet and solemn. Newcomers don't know silence prepares persons for worship; they interpret silence as coldness, so we stress moments of silence during the worship.

At the beginning of worship the pastoral staff makes announcements and engages in give-and-take with the congregation, a lot like black churches. We try to make the service comfortable for those who are not accustomed to church. In numerous ways we try to welcome members and visitors alike. Most persons experience warmth and acceptance.

After the welcome, we say, "We have come here to meet the Lord, let's prepare our hearts." Worship begins with a hymn. Often we move into a selection of several praise songs. The spirit of the service dictates how many songs we sing. With the congregation standing we ask them to speak to those next to them, welcoming them to worship.

Another part of our service we call "Christ in Us." During these brief moments, one of the pastors interviews a few members asking how Christ is at work in their lives. Generally, we have talked to these persons before the service.

On any given Sunday you might hear contemporary choral music or a classical piece. You might also experience a presentation from the drama group or time with the children. Skits and liturgical dance occur with regularity. We make a strong effort to have surprises in every service.

After another hymn, the offertory, or an anthem, we turn to the reading of the scripture. So that everyone may follow the reading, the text is printed in the bulletin. I try to preach the text faithfully so that it addresses the lives of those present.

We do not have a closing hymn after the service. Too often we saw people looking bored or grabbing their purses, so we conclude with music from the choir, a short praise song, or the benediction.

As I reflect on all the changes in our worship, I am grateful that we have been able to include the new generations without losing those who relish traditional forms of worship. How did we manage these changes? Very carefully!

First, we introduced changes gradually. After working with the music director, the choir, and informing the congregation, we made small changes. These changes we called "experiments," assuring the congregation that if it was not a good change we would go back to our traditional forms.

Our youth and children's groups introduced different kinds of music. Children can seldom do anything wrong. For example, we sang the Gloria Patri and then had the children sing a praise song following it. Two styles but the same intention.

Special days like Pentecost or Easter gave us opportunities for experimentation. On Pentecost Sunday we asked people to dress in red; on another Sunday we celebrated our heritage by dressing in tartans.

I thanked people for trying new things; I sympathized with those who sacrificed their tastes and preferences for the sake of another generation. As I think about the changes, we have had a minimum of conflict, our worship has remained Reformed and sound, and our congregation has been able to reach a broad spectrum of persons. (INTERVIEW WITH MARK TOONE, PASTOR, CHAPEL HILL COMMUNITY PRESBYTERIAN CHURCH, GIG HARBOR, WA.)

The proposal for a transitional church calls for re-visioning the worship style common in most mainline congregations. From the perspective of the outsider, traditional worship fails to communicate clearly, to encourage participation, or to speak to deeply felt needs. If we intend to reach the younger generation with the message of Christ, worship must be transformed. Traditional congregations can create new forms of relevant worship in a variety of ways: by imagining an alternative order of worship that embodies the tradition with integrity, by experiencing non-traditional worship, by imagining new forms of the liturgy and evaluating it with respect to aim, style, form, and content, and by defining the role of the minister in an alternative order of worship. The interview with Mark Toone indicates that he and his staff took these steps in their process of change.

IMAGINE AN ALTERNATIVE ORDER OF WORSHIP

What would it be like to attend a service of worship that has few of the traditional elements to which you have become accustomed? Perhaps a description of such a service will spark your imagination.

On the Sunday that you attend this worship service, you are driving to the church at 10:45 a.m. Suddenly you find yourself in a traffic jam more than four miles long. You wonder if there has been an accident. Later, you see flashing blue and red lights on a police car, and that momentarily provides the answer—an accident. But upon getting closer to the lights you realize there has been no accident. The police are directing traffic into a church parking lot.

As you enter the driveway, a man appears on the roof with a walkie-talkie in hand. He is directing the volunteers who are assisting with the parking. About twenty-five persons help members and visitors park. Someone in the vast parking lot welcomes you to the church.

When you exit your car you notice that the building ahead looks more like a sports arena than a church. Streams of people pour into the building from all sides. As you survey the crowd, you are struck by its youthfulness. Most seem to be in their twenties and thirties. They wear jeans and jackets. If they own ties and skirts, they have left them in their BMWs and Mercedes.

The service begins with music from the band. The leader functions like a Mistress of Ceremonies rather than a liturgist. She wears a dress, not a robe. Behind her sits a band with drums, guitars, and a keyboard. The thirty-piece orchestra has been given a day's vacation.

The leader introduces the theme for the morning. She says, "Today we will be talking about admitting to God and to another person the exact nature of our faults."

Once you are seated you begin to survey the "worship" environment. The stage reveals the best equipment with lights, curtains, speakers, a Plexiglas pulpit, and flowers. It looks like a theater or a civic center. You notice stage hands scurrying around, constantly changing the props, getting ready for the next presentation.

The service begins with a chorus. The leader

repeats it several times. The words are simple: "Oh, how he loves you and me — He gave his life; what more could he give? Oh, how he loves you and me." Later, as you reflect, you realize this chorus was the only group song.

Following the group singing, an excellent soloist enlarges on the theme with the words, "Don't Suffer in Silence."

Before the last note fades, a liturgical dancer dramatizes the confession of sin while quoting Psalm 32. Each phrase is punctuated with appropriate gestures, pirouettes, pauses, jumps, and falls. During the three- or four-minute recital, deep feelings arise within you.

When the crowd applauds after each presentation, you sometimes wonder if you are attending a worship service or a concert.

After another musical presentation, two persons offer a six-minute drama. The setting: a high school classroom. Two graduates have returned for a class reunion and they recall their days in this classroom. One of them speaks about the guilt he has felt for abusing a gay classmate, once joining a friend in tying the boy to the radiator and taunting him about his sexual preference. With grief he confesses that the gay student later committed suicide. Facing his guilt and shame, the returning graduate says, "It wasn't right. I'm sorry. I truly am."

Following the drama, the leader steps forward and speaks to the crowd, "I'm giving you a rare gift: silence. Pause and think about what you have seen and heard."

After a few moments, the leader continues with announcements and introduces an offering. She carefully instructs you as a visitor to feel no pressure to give. "You are our guest," she says.

After the offering, the minister arises from the front row of seats, walks to the stage, stands behind the Plexiglas pulpit and speaks on the theme of confession for about forty-five minutes. When he finishes, the service ends — no song, no prayer, no benediction.

As you leave someone says that on a typical weekend, more than twenty thousand persons attend five services like this.

Consider these questions:

1. Why do you suppose 20,000 young men and women attend these services weekly?

2. What aspects of this Sunday service raise questions for you?

3. How might you incorporate changes in your worship service that would reach the younger generation?

4. What problems would a change in the order and content of service present to the members of your congregation?

REFLECT ON THIS ALTERNATIVE SERVICE

An alternative worship experience raises a number of questions — indeed different ones for different people. Some will say it focuses on the subjective experience of the worshipper rather than on the holiness of God. Perhaps there are essential elements missing in this model, but consider those aspects that can feed the imagination of worship leaders in mainline congregations.

1. This worship is "culture specific." Recognizing that those born after 1950 have been formed by television, the worship is visual. It depends on images and actions as much as words. The entertainment atmosphere offers a familiar setting. In harmony with the concert setting, the dress code is Saturday-casual.

2. The form of worship appeals to the senses. The

dramatic and artistic elements in the service engage different senses. If we are to worship God with our whole being, must we not appeal to all the senses? Ancient Jewish and Christian worship appealed to eye, ear, nose, and hand. Incense, vestments, and icons were regular parts of worship and provided a full sensory experience. If these sensory actions no longer communicate with the younger generation, what modern media will communicate the divine presence and enrich the act of worship?

3. Worship follows an entertainment format. *Worship is not entertainment!* True. But for a spectator generation, the stage, the mistress of ceremonies, and the drama in this scenario provide a familiar setting with thought-provoking content that prepares the people for an encounter with God. Is this not better than retaining a form of worship that alienates the unchurched generation?

4. This worship is incarnational. It incarnates in the sense that it borrows the forms of the culture to which the younger generation has become accustomed — music, drama, short bytes, and sharp statements of truth. To reach the "lost" generation we must take seriously their culture. To remain frozen in the liturgies of another age ignores the cultural context and produces a form and style of worship that obscures the gospel of Christ.

5. Worship occurs in the language of participants. While religious language has its place, compassionate churches must build their worship with a sensitivity to participants who do not know the sacred words of the tradition. Theological words can be broken apart with synonyms, short phrases, or a sentence. Take the word "redemption," for example. One can say, "Brought back," or "What God has done through Christ to make things right."

Of what value is speech that is not understood? As a way of taking stock, in just one worship service make a list of words in the bulletin or spoken from the pulpit that would not be understood by a non-church visitor.

7. The style of worship corresponds to the lifestyle of those gathered. Elements in the service flow easily and naturally. Nothing seems manipulative or contrived. The younger generation demands authenticity. The Lucite pulpit provides a "see-through" experience for the congregation, symbolizing the openness and vulnerability of the preacher. The minister has nothing to hide; there is no hocus pocus in the hour of presentation.

8. The sermon answers questions of the people. They want to know how to deal with issues or incidents for which they cannot forgive themselves. The message is applicable and practical.

Based on the fifth step in Alcoholics Anonymous, the minister calls for the confession of one's whole life to another person. He makes a clear presentation: why we need to confess, how we confess, to whom we confess, and the consequences of our confession. In a vulnerable manner the minister relates how he has made a confession of his life.

9. This service demonstrates that Sunday morning worship can be different from the staid, tame, predictable services conducted in most of our sanctuaries. Whether worship should be formed exclusively for the unchurched person raises legitimate questions about the nature and role of worship — but this experience reveals that old, traditional ways of worship can be reformed to speak with clarity, relevance, and power to a new generation.

To create a celebration that reaches the post-1950 generation, we must take seriously the culture that has created its constituents and the lenses through which they view reality. What do you learn from the interview with Mark Toone and from the worship described above? To whom does your worship appeal? Who is being excluded? The new celebration will not be created *de nouveau*, but as a revision of a long, established tradition. Innovations must be made gradually and with sensitivity to all the participants.

CREATE A PERSONAL EXPERIENCE

For a pastor and worship committee to get a better idea of what an alternative worship service looks and feels like, try a first-hand experience. Attend a church that offers an alternative style. In every metropolitan area and in most cities and towns, non-denominational, alternative congregations have sprung up. While not all of these are successful, most of them are filled with the generations that mainline churches have lost. The suggestion to visit one of these churches does not imply that you should embrace without question their form, style, or content. But we should be willing to learn from congregations that prove effective in ways that mainline churches do not. What do you suppose keeps us from attending one of these alternative forms of church? As you investigate how other congregations worship, these suggestions may be of help:

1. Choose the best and most effective church in your area to visit. Try to choose a congregation that might be a bit closer to your own. If none exists in your community, visit one in a nearby city.

2. When you attend this service pay special attention to the following:

— How are you welcomed?

— Who is in attendance?

— What order of worship is followed?

— What type of music is favored? What instruments?

— What mission does the church seem to have?

— What view of the world does the sermon reflect?

— What traditional elements of worship are omitted?

— Do you sense the presence of Christ?

3. Does your experience of this style of worship suggest any changes that should be made in your normal Sunday worship?

4. What objections do you anticipate if you change

your style of worship? How can you make these changes with the least amount of conflict or confusion?

What Happens at Your Church On Sunday Morning?

One way to evaluate your Sunday morning worship with respect to the "lost" generation would be to attend the service with the mind-set of a non-churched person under fifty years of age. Write a careful description of your reactions to what occurs and from the perspective of a first-time visitor. (Better yet, enlist a couple of sensitive, discerning, and or articulate non-churched persons to do this task for you. It would be worth paying them for their efforts!) The results of either of these evaluations will be enlightening!

What is Sunday morning about? Perhaps some adults derive more good from Sunday morning than we recognize — even some of those born after 1950. But surveys suggest that the culture of Sunday morning stands in sharp contrast with the secular culture of twenty- to fifty-year-olds. Whether their memory of church leaves them cold, or their recent experience of worship turns them off, these persons are notably absent from most of our churches.

What do you think occurs for most persons who worship at your church on a given Sunday?

What happens to visitors who attend, but do not return?

What will persons born after 1950 experience when they return to worship in your congregation?

How to Rethink Your Liturgy

Let us assume that you have been open to the judgment that many of our worship services do not afford easy access for persons under fifty years of age. Recognizing this fact will not produce change. We need a process for revising the liturgy in a way that retains its integrity and also makes it possible for uninitiated persons to worship.

To evaluate the liturgy, first spend time discussing the question, "What is the role of the liturgy?" A few suggestions may stimulate and focus your conversation.

If we strip away all liturgical form and closely inspect the intent of Sunday morning, what do we find? What is worship about? Is not worship about the encounter with God? In this hour, the Creator meets the people; the people respond to the divine presence. More goes on, but at the core of worship stands this divine/human encounter that issues in praise, confession, forgiveness, and instruction. God initiates the meeting and humans respond with praise and thanksgiving. We strive to find ways that this encounter may occur with integrity and relevance.

Reforming the liturgy does not begin *de nouveau*. For centuries the people of God have been worshipping and they have refined a way of worship that assists us in becoming aware of God's presence and offering God praise. How do mainline congregations shape a liturgy from the richness of the tradition so that it speaks to the present cultural expectations, values, and social conditioning of the post-1950 generation? The essential components of the liturgy have been hammered out on the anvil of the church's experience for two millennia. Again and again the form of the liturgy has been reheated in the furnace of truth and shaped so that worship is conducted with integrity and relevance in a new cultural situation. Our worship needs an immersion in the Spirit that can be fused with contemporary culture to create a meaning-link with a new generation.

The recreation of an appropriate liturgy must be the work of a particular people. The form of the liturgy does not come off the drawing board of worship architects, but it arises out of the praise of worshipping congregations. It must be incarnational, that is, shaped by the gospel and the culture in which worship occurs. True worship must be born out of the culture, according to scripture, informed by tradition, and guided by the Spirit. Consider thoughtfully these four components: culture, scripture, tradition, and Holy Spirit. Bearing in mind these constitutive elements, we may envision an appropriate liturgy for worship.

According to these four norms, reflect on the movements in worship and imagine alternative ways to fill them. These alterations must have integrity with the tradition and scripture, respond to the culture, and open up the congregation's communion with God.

To provide more variety in worship, suggest that the changes be gradual and that they communicate a deeper awareness of God. This imaginative work should be done by a group that includes the minister, older members of the congregation, and participants in cell groups.

The following presents one form of liturgy with suggestions for creating an alternative order of worship. This guide may assist you in evaluating, imagining, and reconstructing your worship in a form that invites those outside the faith to learn the message of the gospel and to respond to this gracious offer of God. The form of the liturgy we have chosen includes Gathering in God's Presence, Listening for God, Responding to God's Word, Celebrating the Word, and Incarnating the Word.

GATHERING IN GOD'S PRESENCE

The gathering draws us out of our routine concerns and into God's presence. Each aspect of the gathering helps us make the conscious transition from our ordinary time and space into sacred time and space.

The gathering traditionally includes a musical prelude, a sung or spoken prayer invoking God's presence, hymns of praise, prayers of confession, assurance of pardon, and an affirmation of faith. As the people of God gather before the Creator, these have always been the forms of the initial divine/human encounter.

Questions to consider:

1. How does your congregation gather in the presence of God? How effectively does the present form call forth the awareness of God? For whom is it meaningful? Whom does it ignore?

2. What form of music best communicates with new persons you seek to reach?

3. How may persons be invited into an awareness of the divine presence to help them attend to God during worship?

4. How can persons be invited to express their praise to God in new and more participative ways?

5. What historic or contemporary confessions can help the congregation to say what it truly believes? Could the congregation write its own confession?

6. What do you learn about a different style in the interview at the beginning of the chapter?

LISTENING FOR GOD

In this aspect of worship, the people give attention to the voice of God. Worshippers listen for God through scripture (both Old and New Testaments), anthems, and the sermon.

Consider these questions as a way of evaluating your present form of worship.

1. Does your present order of worship cause people to expect God to speak?

2. How can scripture be read with greater reverence and clarity? Do you provide silence for persons to reflect on the text?

3. Should different members be encouraged to read the scripture?

4. What type anthem appeals to the membership? To new persons who worship with you? To persons you would like to reach?

5. How can you provide an atmosphere of warmth in the leadership of worship?

6. How can preaching be more intentional in speaking the word of God to the people? Consider language, style, and content.

7. How can persons be encouraged to speak of God's activity in their lives?

RESPONDING TO GOD'S WORD

In our response during worship, we open our lives more deeply to God, offer ourselves, our prayers, intercessions, and financial means to God. Perhaps these questions will help you assess your response to God.

1. How effectively does the present order of worship lead persons to respond to God with praise, commitment, intercession, and finances?

2. To what extent is silence a vital part of your worship of God?

3. What opportunities are given for persons to make personal responses to the call of God?

4. Are there invitations to respond to God in prayer, in conversation with the minister, in a commitment of the heart to God?

5. Do persons realize that making an offering symbolizes the dedication of themselves to God?

CELEBRATING THE WORD

The Lord's table provides the most intimate worship of God. In the Eucharist we receive the body and blood of Christ; he nourishes the life of the Spirit within us; he lives in us and we in him. Celebrating the sacrament "enacts" the Word of God in visible and tangible forms.

Consider these questions as you evaluate your present communion.

1. How often do you offer the Lord's Supper?

2. To what extent do members anticipate, prepare for, and expect to receive Christ in the sacrament of the Lord's Supper? How can all members be better prepared to receive Christ through the sacrament?

3. Evaluate different ways to receive the sacrament. Receive the sacrament in the pew, at the altar, around the table, in a family circle; offer the elements to each other. Try ways other than your present tradition.

'INCARNATING' THE WORD

Worship brings glory to God and transforms our lives so that we may flesh out this transformative word in daily life. The benediction communicates the blessing and presence of God upon the people. They go from worship to live for him who died and rose again.

Collect your creative imaginings.

Prioritize the changes you plan to make and introduce them in an orderly manner.

EVALUATE YOUR PROPOSAL

When you have prepared a revised order of worship, evaluate it from the perspective of aim, style, content, and form. These perspectives offer yet another way to evaluate and revise your present worship. With the insights gained from your research and evaluation, initiate changes.

Review the aim. The weekly celebration brings together people to worship God. Worship is not entertainment, nor positive reinforcement, nor a marketplace to display and dispense faith. Rather, the worship celebration provides sacred space to worship Almighty God. Other things occur in the celebration, but worship centers upon God. With respect to non-churched persons, nothing will be more compelling than a community that knows God and worships with reverence, energy, and faithfulness.

Review the form. By form we mean boundaries and progression. In part, form refers to day and hour, the sacred time and place. Sunday, for many, will remain the only day for public worship, but the resurrection, which made every day holy and all time sacred, liberates us to consider other days for worship. So worship can be on Saturday or Thursday; it can be at 7 p.m., as well as 11 a.m. Should you consider a different time and place?

Form also means the progression of worship — gathering, responding to God, celebrating, listening for God, departing in faith. But remember form can be altered according to the context and the needs of persons. Leaders of worship should insure that persons understand the movement of worship and how best to participate.

Form can also denote the role of the leader and the extent to which participation is encouraged. Be attentive to the degree persons participate in or remain spectators. Participation can be in spirit as well as in action.

Review the style. Style points to "how" and "in what manner" the celebration takes place. Style refers especially to music. In an inclusive celebration, the music cannot be limited to the three B's — Bach, Beethoven, and Brahms. Persons unschooled in classical music do not understand the language of the great composers. Organ chords sound strange to persons who have listened to guitars, drums, and keyboards all week.

Style also indicates the quality of music, sermon, and leadership. The modern generation has no patience with ill-planned and poorly executed worship; it demands quality in both content and leadership. Our opening illustration indicates how one church strives for excellence.

Language must be included in style. Does your proposed style of worship use a language understandable to outsiders? Understandable language does not require you to expunge religious words from the vocabulary of worship. But sensitivity to language does lead to gender-inclusive speaking and short explanations of unfamiliar words.

Review the content. What marks the substance of your worship? Is there a clear recognition of God's presence? Does the form of worship encourage persons to offer prayer and praise to God?

Is the word of God given centrality? Is space provided to listen? Do persons hear the gospel in song, story, and drama?

A FINAL WORD

The need to reach a generation lost to the mainline churches drives the redesign of worship. Many of these "drop-outs" are returning to the church in search of answers to their life-sized questions. Since the worship service provides the first contact most of them will have with the church, a welcoming environment is crucial.

If you have no opportunity or intention to reach the generation born after 1950, do not bother to change your form of worship. You will only succeed in enraging those who have worshipped the same way for 40 years. But, if you do intend to reach the unchurched of this generation, change is imperative!

CHAPTER 9

How to Liberate the Laity

Ten years ago 10 percent of the membership was doing 90 percent of the work. Most loyal members were burned out, defensive, and angry about the overload. A new pastor came who said, "We must change the way we do church; we need a new vision and a new plan of ministry. Our present way of 'doing church' feels more like a business than a community of faith; we must change this approach."

The leadership pulled together nine persons, kicking and screaming, and began to explore the kinds of changes our situation demanded. Out of those conversations came a clear vision of who we were called to be, an identity — and based on this identity we adopted a few achievable goals.

Our first goal was to transform the organization into a community, a community of caring. A caring community responds to those who need care and directs to places of ministry those who have care to give. Getting those who "have" with those who "need" gave birth to my call as the Director of Lay Ministry. My task was to get 80 percent of the congregation involved in caring and ministering instead of merely 10 percent.

My frustrations included issues of language, role models, plus styles, and sources of instruction. Most of the information I found describing work with volunteers came from secular sources and did not translate easily into ministry in the church. After two years of struggling with this translation I discovered a book, **How to Mobilize**

Church Volunteers by Marlene Wilson. In a few chapters she answered questions I had muddled through for months. She, a church woman by commitment, had worked in secular organizations and had translated their insights into the language of faith.

As my vision became clearer, my church did not readily embrace it because the new vision called for enormous changes in established practices. The resistance I experienced would have overwhelmed me had it not been for a minister who knew how to enable a lay woman. With his encouragement and support I survived. We had our first significant breakthrough into a significant lay ministry with a group of new members.

We discovered that change came easier with new persons than with established members, so we focused our efforts on each group of new members. We began with an emphasis on gifts and giftedness. We challenged new persons and the larger congregation to make their gifts available to others, to show their caring. A number of persons responded to this initiative.

We then restructured the new member classes. The minister taught five hours on faith, doctrine, and the history of the denomination. I taught about giftedness and the use of time, talent, and money. I issued specific challenges for ministry in and through the church. I encouraged the new members to say "no" until they found their specific call. Furthermore, I urged them not to try to give care if they were in great need of care. I have learned an important lesson, "There is a time to serve and there is a time to be served." In response to this new member training, numerous ministries got started.

As various ministries through the new members began to bloom, we discovered that many of

*our former officers felt used, neglected, and out-
side the communication loop. To respond to their
alienation we formed "The Fellowship of the
Ordained." When officers ended a term we conducted an exit interview to help us evaluate their
experience as an officer, especially whether their
expectations had been met. This group met regularly for coffee and conversation. Soon they
became a group of advisors who tested new decisions and offered suggestions for future planning.
In this way we avoided their feeling ignored, dis-
connected, and unappreciated.*

*Once the vision of lay ministry began to take
root in the congregation, our caring expressed
itself in sponsors for new members, through fellowship and nurture in classes, small groups,
and in retreats. We have reached outside the
church to scores of persons in need. In ten years
our church has changed from being pastor- and
staff-dominated to a community of involved, caring laity. During this period our membership has
tripled to about 1,100 and our attendance has
increased by an even greater percentage.*
(INTERVIEW WITH SUE MALLORY, DIRECTOR,
LEADERSHIP TRAINING NETWORK)

Every congregation desires to overcome the stalemate
created by having twenty percent of the people do eighty
percent of the work and give most of the money. This situation, so firmly embedded in the culture of most mainline congregations, requires a new type of leadership in
the minister and a challenging vision that transforms the
mission of the church. The raw material for this vision
can be found in scripture. With the inspiration of the
Spirit and the wisdom of those who have worked at renewal for decades, liberating the laity for ministry can be
implemented in every congregation.

Liberating the laity requires first a vision and then equipping. Affirming the giftedness of all the baptized marks one starting point. Sue Mallory discovered that those who newly entered the life of the church had an openness to hearing this message. But the affirmation of gifts must be followed by challenging opportunities to use them. These challenges may come through the ministry of the church or they may arise in the discernment of small groups. Opportunities for ministry may also present themselves in the ordinary relationships of life. Most persons, between the awareness of gifts and the challenge to serve, require equipping for their ministry. Good training provides skills and increases confidence.

A liberated laity functions in the organizational structure of the congregation, in the outreach of the congregation, with individuals in the congregation, and in their worldly vocations. Charles M. Olsen, a church renewalist who has worked on vitality in governance, recognized that many lay leaders were burned out, lacked enthusiasm, and vowed never to serve on a board again. Many left their office disappointed that their service had not been personally rewarding or spiritually challenging.

Olsen suggests that the table of governance bears a similarity to the table of communion. With this high view of leadership he urges leaders to see themselves not as political representatives but as spiritual leaders of the congregation; they are the people of God in community, not managers of programs. Church meetings themselves should be conducted as "worship work" within a structure similar to Sunday morning.[1] To transform the board room into the Upper Room will require conviction, vision, and wise leadership.

In addition to serving in official structures of the church, liberated laity function in mission beyond the organizational structures of the church. Soup kitchens, night shelters, and Habitat for Humanity illustrate some of the ministries of a liberated laity.

The one-to-one ministry of laity takes the form of friendship, spiritual companionship, and mentorship. Some already engaged in this spiritual work would be shocked to hear themselves called a mentor or spiritual companion. Those who have this ministry often slide into it gradually. They become involved in a depth of sharing and caring for others long before they recognize their value to them. They continue in this personal ministry, convicted of its meaning for the recipients.

Finally, the church needs once again to underscore the ministry of persons in their secular vocations. Too often we give persons the impression that valid ministry only happens within or under the auspices of the church, thus diminishing their work in the world. Whether teacher, doctor, lawyer; or carpenter, policeman, plumber; or husband, wife, parent, all the baptized are called to fulfill their vocation in the service of Christ.

The liberated laity have been baptized into Jesus Christ; they have been called to serve him in their work. They serve in the structures of the church as members of his body; with fellow believers they offer his compassion in deeds of love and justice; they spend themselves in listening and caring for fellow members of the Body of Christ; and, they recognize their calling to re-present Christ in home and family, in work and recreation, and in society and civil government.

The preparation for this life of ministry in Jesus Christ receives its original impulse from the Spirit of God, the one who creates and calls persons into a living relationship with God. The small group provides a setting in which lay men and women discover their gifts, develop skills for Christian ministry, and receive nurture and encouragement; the small group also serves as a paradigm of the church, a living community of love and grace. All these benefits for the ministry of the laity underscore the importance of multiplying healthy groups. Finally, regular worship offers praise to God but it also reminds all the members of their true calling as servants of Jesus.

Only when laity receive empowerment for ministry can the church move out powerfully in mission. Although we do not propose to offer a training manual for each role, we will set forth fundamental principles for empowering a liberated laity. These principles have application to small group development, lay training, mission outreach, and evangelism. We will explain each principle and illustrate how it applies to lay ministry.

GROUND MINISTRY IN BIBLICAL TRUTH

All ministry must be grounded in scripture. Biblical truth must be faithfully studied in a relevant manner so that it may be understood and appropriated by lay men and women. Biblical truth, faithfully taught, creates a world view, defines the nature of God, and points toward the fulfillment of God's plan. Scripture makes clear the role of humans in the plan of God.

The biblical view of the world challenges the secular, relativized view held by many today. Its message confronts relativism with a witness to one supreme God who existed before all things, created the world, and providentially directs it. According to the Bible, life and history have not been left to chance.

The Bible refines our vision of God. All persons have an image of God, but it is often perverted. Persons either take God too lightly as a grand old man upstairs or they see God as a heavy-handed judge, or an impersonal energy in the universe. The scriptures give witness to a personal God who knows us, cares for us, and faithfully guides our lives.

But the Bible not only witnesses to God; it mediates an encounter with God. The words of scripture become the word of God *to us*. The human hunger for meaning ultimately finds its satisfaction in this encounter with God through the gospel that speaks the good news of forgiveness and hope. Its message creates a new identity and lifestyle.

Biblical truth may be taught in classes, studied in groups, proclaimed in worship, or read in private. Every encounter with the text both informs and transforms people's lives.

WELCOME INQUIRY FROM OUTSIDERS

Secular, non-churched people need an opportunity to make honest inquiry into the faith. Some fear that "if we open the door for serious inquiry, these secular persons may ask questions we cannot answer." An honest encounter between persons of faith and searching persons can be an enriching experience for both. In the give-and-take of open inquiry, seekers find answers and believers have their faith challenged and deepened. The ability to converse with these inquirers must be part of the equipping of the laity.

To communicate intelligently, laity must learn the language of the non-churched. Those who do not speak in theological categories like *God, church, salvation,* and *forgiveness* need help in giving names to their experiences. They simply do not know the language of the faith, so they neither speak in these categories nor do they understand our insider terms. Their ignorance challenges the laity to translate their witness to God into understandable words.

Given a friendly ear, persons both inside and outside the church will ask basic questions like: "How do I know there is a God? Does God matter? Do I matter to God? How do I make contact with God? How do I deal with serious disappointments in my life?"

Searching persons require a personal, vulnerable response from both clergy and laity. Secular persons have a keen nose for phoniness, so we must rid ourselves of trite cliches and easy answers. Perhaps we will be driven back again and again to telling our own stories of faith in new and fresh ways.

Welcoming inquiry and encouraging tolerance will create in us the spirit of our Lord. Recall John the Baptist's question: "Are you the Christ or do we look for another?" Jesus neither chided nor condemned John for asking this profound question. When a foreign woman argued with Jesus about healing her daughter, Jesus graciously responded to her request. He calls us to tolerate the language, behavior, lifestyle, music, and ideas of those alien to the dominant culture. We begin our work with persons where they are and not where we are.

CREATE EXPOSURE OPPORTUNITIES

This principle derives from Jesus' emphasis on having the disciples "with him." Faith and vision are better caught than taught. To conceive faith in persons, get them in touch with people contagious with faith. The way of Christ is learned through the give-and-take of life together in the church and in friendships.

The contagion principle stands behind our insistence upon creating a vital core of committed disciples at the center of the church's life. The fellowship of love and faith in this group provides a setting for persons to "catch" faith. Members of the core group who have been grounded in scripture develop an open, loving relationship in the Spirit that makes them contagious bearers of the faith.

The exposure principle offers a way of spreading the small group's vitality throughout the congregation. This approach can be limited only by one's imagination: fellowship gatherings, co-teaching, mission projects, hosts, ushers, and committees. When seeking to awaken the gifts of care, witness, or compassionate service, place the awakened with the "not-yet-awake."

The principle of being "with" persons applies also to the ministry of laity in secular vocations. An attorney, for example, invites a fellow attorney to a luncheon where faith is shared. A carpenter invites an assistant to a men's dinner at the church. A teacher invites a fellow teacher to have coffee with her with the conviction that Christ often speaks through their encounter. When the faith of lay men and women has been awakened through the principle of exposure, they naturally employ this approach when reaching out to another person.

Demonstrate Sensitivity to the Culture

Missionaries know that the culture creates the receptors for the gospel. To be faithful, the missionary must understand, identify with, and communicate through the culture of the persons they seek to reach. We cannot expect persons outside the church to embrace Christian culture, language, and theological persuasions before they have become believers. Thus, helpful conversations must be carried on in the culture of the receiver.

Being sensitive to the culture of the other opens the door to satisfactory communication. For example, conversations with youth will demand talk about their concerns — drugs, alcohol, sex, parental conflicts, and peer approval. Communication will break down if adults impose their issues upon the youth.

When a business woman seeks to communicate with a client, she might begin with a common knowledge of business practices and move into the arena of values and ethics. The distance between business and faith narrows with a shift to ethics and core values. To ignore the gap between Christian faith and secular culture renders communication impossible.

The Art of Christian Conversation

Christian faith through the ages has been passed from one person to another through personal witness. In nearly twenty centuries the church has found no more effective method. Parents talk with children about Christ;

friends speak with each other; business persons and civic leaders speak naturally of Christ to associates; ministers of compassion share food, comfort, and conversation.

Christian communication outside the walls of the church depends upon an awakened, liberated laity. In contrast with the notion that polite persons do not talk about religion, many non-church persons will talk with a sensitive listener about the pain of their lives. To respond sensitively to this opportunity, laity need to become good, Christian conversationalists. The church must teach lay men and women to speak naturally of their faith.

If people learn to converse *by conversing*, liberated laity must look for natural opportunities to speak with people about God. Do not moments over coffee, lunches, business trips, and long commuter rides provide time for conversation? Do not committee meetings, Sunday school classes, and informal Christian gatherings provide these natural settings in the church?

Lay persons will be encouraged by hearing others speak of their faith. Introduce to the congregation women and men who speak of Christ in a natural, attractive, compelling manner. Invite them to speak to fellowship dinners, Sunday school classes, or even a worship service. One positive model exceeds in value a week of instruction.

Complement these strong role models with good instruction. Books, audio and video tapes, and modular teaching programs have flooded the market with helpful ways to share the faith.

Affirm Human Worth

Many persons struggle with feelings of inadequacy. Their gifts remain frozen because they do not believe their efforts matter to others. Feelings of uselessness keep them from speaking, even when they have something of value to say. A single word of encouragement may free persons for a transforming ministry. These three affirmations have helped many to use their gifts:

1. "God can use your life." Many Christians think of themselves as having nothing to offer anyone. God could use Paul or Peter or Mother Teresa, but not them. Throughout history God has done extraordinary things with very ordinary people when they trusted God's power above their own.

2. "God will use your life now as at no other time." When confronted with the opportunity to serve a fellow human being or speak a word of encouragement or listen to a painful story, these persons often think of their own failures and needs. How can they speak to another or reach out with hope when they feel their own imperfections? If only they were not struggling with a personal problem, or if they were praying more, or if their lives were "together" better, God could use them.

I am convinced that God can use the woundedness of persons to minister to others. Their struggles, failures, and problems provide the connecting points. "We help persons more through our weaknesses than through our strengths." Our experiences today provide the best material for connecting with others. Honest sharing of our present needs builds bridges. Never again will we have this present story to tell, life to share, or pain to expose. Therefore, God can use us today as at no other time.

3. "You are the best Christian somebody knows." Despite the flaws in our faith and the imperfection of our lives, each of us is Christ's best representative to someone. What a challenging thought! Let us pray that we may be faithful to this person who drinks in our influence.

The capacity of liberated lay persons deepens as they mature in the faith. As they draw closer to God they learn to see God in all of life, to view life through eyes of faith, and to live with the confidence that God is in all things.

Experience Faith

A culture demanding emotional expression and personal involvement must be invited to experience the faith, not merely hear about it. This generation wants more than neat theological presentations on Sunday morning; they want to see personal demonstrations of faith in daily life. Authentic expressions of compassion and caring intensify their longing for the living God.

The experience of God often comes into a person's awareness when he or she least expects it. These surprise intrusions into persons' lives may represent the lever that pries open their minds. Traumatic experiences also open persons to an awareness of God. Near-death experiences, accidents, great joy, loss, divorce, a serious illness — all these human experiences tend to shake persons out of complacency. In the moment of profound self-awareness, God breaks into our consciousness and creates "newness." Being aware of the potential in these moments should make every lay minister sensitive to persons in transition.

Invite persons to become aware of God. In conversations with persons about their lives, wonder with them about life's meaning. A man drinks coffee with a fellow employee and in the course of conversation his friend speaks of disappointment over not getting a promotion. The Christian conversationalist says, "I wonder what that means." If the disappointed friend picks up on his response, he may later ask, "Where do you think God might be in this missed opportunity?" Wondering and questioning invites a person to look at the larger meaning of his or her life.

Progressive Commitment

For the most part, mainline churches have hesitated to ask persons to make serious commitments to Jesus

Christ. We find it easier to embrace the culture than to challenge it. Evidence from conservative churches indicates that persons want to be challenged; they want to give themselves to something that demands sacrifice. Christ never hesitated to issue challenges for radical change: "Come, follow me." "Sell what you have and give to the poor, and come follow me."

Even when confronted with a radical challenge, persons respond in degrees — awareness, interest, exploration, testing, partial commitment, deeper commitment. The ways in which persons become aware of their need for God are almost limitless. Often the awareness begins with a need for friendship. Sometimes it comes when life caves in and dreams die. At other times the awakening comes through a sermon, a witness, a tragedy, emptiness, a book, a need to find someone to thank for their blessings.

A spiritual awakening stimulates interest. The interest may be nothing more than curiosity. Other awakened persons will show interest by speaking with a friend, going to church, or buying a book. Interest often expresses itself in questions.

Interest leads to exploration. Tentatively this newly awakened person may watch a worship service on television, speak with a friend, or attend a Bible class. In these various settings an awakened person asks questions, considers options, and builds up the courage to make a decision for Christ.

Seeking individuals test options to determine what is appropriate. Testing measures the depth of commitment required, the risk involved, and the possibility of continuing in a new way of life. This commitment creates a new identity—a disciple of Jesus Christ.

At some point, either suddenly or gradually, searching persons make a commitment. They commit as much of themselves as they can to as much of Christ as they understand.

From this conscious beginning in a life of discipleship,

the new Christian later will be involved in deeper and deeper commitments to God's will and purpose.

INVITE

Able lay ministers extend invitations to others. They learn to use the phrase, "I invite you . . ." Through their loving service, their diligent listening, and their gift of compassion, they issue verbal invitations. Just a slight shift can make a spectator a seeker. Consider these invitations:

☀ I invite you to consider what Christ might mean to your life. (awakening)

☀ I invite you to think how fellowship with Christians might enrich your life. (interest)

☀ I invite you to look at all the options for your life before you decide for Christ. (exploration)

☀ I invite you to imagine what it would be like to entrust your life to Christ. (testing)

☀ I invite you to give as much of yourself as you can to Christ. (beginning commitment)

MATURE SPIRITUAL GUIDES

Mentorship has deep roots in the biblical tradition. Jesus chose twelve to follow him. He demonstrated to them his mission; he taught them and later explained the meaning of the message; he sent them out to participate in his ministry; he received their reports and encouraged them. The apostles used the same method of developing workers.

Barnabas mentored Paul and Paul guided Timothy. In the biblical record mature persons in the faith adopted younger disciples and supervised their growth. Disciples learned through observation and imitation.

In recent years this ancient way of spiritual guidance

has received increased attention. The practice goes by many names: spiritual direction, soul friend, spiritual friend, spiritual guide, and companion on the inner way. In this relationship one person becomes the mentor of another. To expand the number of these spiritual mentors and to equip them for mature ministry, we need to become more deliberate in the identification and encouragement of these lay ministers of Christ.

MISSIONAL APPLICATION

These principles may be incorporated in committee meetings, Sunday school classes, personal relationships, or worship services. Consider, for example, the application of these principles in the formation of mission groups.

Groups are grounded in scripture. Leaders encourage persons to bring their questions for discussion. The group provides a vital center for exposing marginal or unchurched persons to serious discipleship. Healthy groups provide safe places for secular persons to raise questions because members are sensitive to the secular culture and willing to be challenged by it. In a safe environment both church leaders and inquirers learn to speak naturally of Christ. In the group, persons encounter God through worship, scripture, and faith sharing. Weekly persons feel the challenge to deeper levels of commitment. And in the maturing life of group members qualities of spiritual guidance are being developed.

Epilogue

We stand at the threshold of a New Day — and we are compelled by the example of Jesus of Nazareth to step into it with eyes open to the culture about us. To do this means risk. Change. Grieving what is left behind to embrace what lies ahead. And yet we must do so, in obedience to the Spirit of Christ.

Like the men, women, and children on Managua's Roosevelt Boulevard, we must determine the soundness of the structures of establishment in which we gather — and whether to play nonchalantly in the courtyards of decay, or to press ahead and reconstruct what has been devastated by a cultural shake-up.

The issues are real. The stakes are high. The models are do-able. The choices are ours.

Appendix A

The following guidelines provide a simple, clear, meaningful approach to praying more effectively. Different groups of persons will find theses suggestions helpful, e.g., ministers, elders, Sunday school classes, retreat participants, circles, prayer and sharing groups.

Introduction of the emphasis on prayer

The minister (or other designated leader) invites persons in the congregation to covenant together to pray seriously for the church and for their own lives over the next month. Participants should plan to meet six times for instruction and reporting on their progress. Each person should bring a copy of *New Day, New Church* to the meeting, as well as a notebook for recording observations and experiences.

SESSION 1

Invite the participants to write "an autobiography of prayer." Include in these reflections:

1) Times when prayer was meaningful in my life

2) Ways I have prayed

3) Problems I have had or do have with prayer

4) Hopes I have for this new experience with prayer.

In plenary or small groups give persons the opportunity to discuss their "autobiography."

Review the approach to corporate prayer. Instruct the group to study this approach to prayer and put insights into practice at the next worship service.

SESSION 2

Lead a time of sharing on the experience of corporate prayer. Questions to consider:

1) What effect did praying the liturgy have on my worship experience?

2) What aspect of the liturgy was particularly significant to me?

3) What problems did I have with trying to stay in an attitude of prayer?

4) What difference would it make in the service if 50 percent of the members prayed the liturgy together?

Review the suggestions for personal prayer. Invite the group to pray in this manner for the next week and be prepared to report on their experiences at the next meeting.

To assist in the reporting, ask each person to record in a note-book:

1) The time I have set aside for prayer each day

2) The place I have chosen as a place of prayer

3) The experiences I have each day during my prayer time.

SESSION 3

Begin the session with a report on personal prayer. Deal with issues and problems that arise.

Review the suggestions for life-centered prayer. Encourage the members of the group to reflect on their lives at least three days in the coming week and record their answers to the following questions:

1) What was God saying to me in this event?

2) What am I being called to do?

3) How does this event connect with the rest of my life?

4) What hints about my future does this event hold?

SESSION 4

Begin the session with a report on life-centered prayer.

Review the suggestions for bonding prayer.

Invite the members of the class to choose partners for whom they will pray daily. (You may open this experience to the whole congregation by asking them to draw names or choose a prayer partner for the week.) Invite each person to pray for the other in the four ways we have suggested: 1) in one's own words; 2) in God's words; 3) in spontaneous words; 4) prayer in images.

SESSION 5

Hear reports of the experiences in praying for another.

Introduce Quiet Prayer. Since this form of prayer may be new to the participants, it is recommended that they follow the suggestions for the first time as a group.

The leader guides the group through the seven steps outlined earlier in the section Quiet Prayer. After completing step six, the group should remain in silence for twenty minutes.

After the period of silence, time must be given for verbal reflection on the group's experience.

SESSION 6

Open the session by inviting reports on the experience of Quiet Prayer during the past week.

Since this is the final meeting, it is an appropriate time to evaluate the overall impact of the prayer emphasis. Use the following questions for reflection.

1) How has this prayer experiment affected me? The group with which I have been working? Our congregation?

2) What steps do we need to take to deepen and expand the life of prayer in our whole congregation?

3) Who in our congregation may be called by God to get training in the area of prayer and spiritual life?

4) How can we assist these persons in fulfilling their call?

Appendix B

For more information on effectively liberating lay persons, contact the following persons.

Dr. E. Stanley Ott
Vital Churches Institute, Inc.
Box 18378
Pittsburgh, PA 15236

Rev. Glenn McDonald
Zionsville Presbyterian Church
4775 W. 116th Street
Zionsville, IN 46077

Ms. Sue Mallory
LEAD
8142 Billowvista Drive
Playa del Rey, CA 90293

NOTES

Chapter 1

1 Robert G. Kempler, "A History of the United Church of Christ 1957-2007," *Colleague*, April 1992. Telepax, St. Joseph, MI 49085.

2 Dietrich Bonhoeffer, *Life Together* (New York: Harper and Row, 1954), p.21.

3 David J. Bosch, *Transforming Mission* (Maryknoll, NY: Orbis Books, 1991), p. 114.

4 Hendrikus Berkhof, *The Doctrine of the Holy Spirit* (Atlanta: John Knox Press, 1976).

5 Eugene Peterson, *Earth and Altar* (Downers Grove, IL: InterVarsity Press, 1985), p. 49.

6 Bosch, *Transforming Mission*, p. 114.

7 George G. Hunter III, *How to Reach Secular People* (Nashville: Abingdon, 1992), p. 73.

8 Lesslie Newbigin, *The Gospel in a Pluralist Society* (Grand Rapids, MI: William B. Eerdmanns, 1989), p. 136.

9 Martin Hengel, *Property and Riches in the Early Church* (Philadelphia: Fortress Press, 1974), p. 65.

10 Newbigin, *The Gospel in a Pluralist Society*, p. 243.

Chapter 2

1 Samuel Shoemaker, *The Conversion of the Church* (New York: Fleming H. Revell, 1932).

2 Loren B. Mead, *The Once and Future Church* (Washington, D.C.: The Alban Institute, 1991), p. 43.

3 Jurgen Moltmann, *The Church in the Power of the Spirit* (New York: Harper & Row, 1975), p. 241.

4 Hunter, *How to Reach Secular People*, p. 44.

5 William Easum, *Dancing with Dinosaurs* (Nashville: Abingdon Press, 1993), p. 49.

6 *Ibid.*, p. 54.

7 Bosch, *Transforming Mission*, p. 263.

8 Newbigin, *The Gospel in a Pluralist Society*, p. 7.

9 Hunter, *How to Reach Secular People*, p. 106.

10 Leith Anderson, *Dying for Change* (Minneapolis: Bethany House, 1994), p. 85.

11 Tex Sample, *U.S. Lifestyles and Mainline Churches* (Louisville, KY: John Knox Press, 1990), p. 17.

12 Leith Anderson, *A Church for the 21st Century* (Minneapolis, MN: Bethany House Publishers, 1992) .

13 E. Stanley Ott, *Vision for a Vital Church* (Decatur, GA: CTS Press, 1994).

14 Bosch, *Transforming Mission*, p. 3.

15 Allan Bloom, *The Closing of the American Mind* (New York: Simon and Schuster, 1987), pp. 60, 131.

16 *Ibid.*, p. 56.

17 Dorothy Sayers, *Creed or Chaos?* (New York: Harcourt Brace, 1949), p. 7.

18 Easum, *Dancing with Dinosaurs*, p. 52.

Chapter 3

1 Hunter, *How to Reach Secular People*, pp. 42-43.

2 *Ibid.*, p. 43.

3 *Ibid.*, p.44.

4 Quoted in Hunter, *How to Reach Secular People*, p. 56.

5 "Mainline Churches: The Real Reason for Decline," *First Things* March 1993, p. 18.

6 Robert Bellah, et al., *Habits of the Heart* (Berkely, CA: University of California Press, 1985), p. 144.

7 Tex Sample, *U.S. Lifestyles and Mainline Churches*, pp. 11-14.

8 Hunter, *How to Reach Secular People*, p. 45.

9 *Ibid.*, p. 46.

10 Easum, *Dancing with Dinosaurs*, p. 55.

11 Hunter, *How to Reach Secular People*, pp. 49ff.

12 Loren B. Mead, *Transforming Congregations for the Future* (Washington, D.C.: Alban Institute, 1994), p. 48.

Chapter 4

1 Mead, *The Once and Future Church*, p. 43.

2 Edward Dixon Junkin, "Up From the Grass Roots, the Church in Transition," *Interpretation*, July 1992, vol. XLVI No. 9, p. 273.

3 See Carl F. George, *Prepare Your Church for the Future* (Tarrytown, NY: Fleming H. Revell, 1991); William Easum,

Dancing With Dinosaurs (Nashville: Abingdon Press, 1993);
and Leith Anderson, *A Church for the 21st Century*
(Minneapolis, MN: Bethany House Publishers, 1992).

Chapter 5

1 This concept of ministry is spelled out in E. Stanley Ott, *Vision for a Vital Church* (Decatur, GA: CTS Press, 1994).

2 See Loren B. Mead, *The Once and Future Church.*

3 Ott, *Vision for a Vital Church.*

4 For help in preparing leaders for this task, see Robert H. Ramey, Jr., *Growing Church Leaders* (Decatur, GA: CTS Press, 1995).

5 See Ben Johnson, *95 Theses for the Church* (Decatur, GA: CTS Press, 1995) for a more detailed discussion.

6 Mead, *The Once and Future Church*, pp. 71-80.

7 See Charles M. Olsen, *Transforming Church Boards into Communities of Spiritual Leaders* (Washington, D.C.: The Alban Institute, 1995).

Chapter 6

1 See Ben Johnson, *To Will God's Will* (Philadelphia: The Westminster Press, 1987), p. 109. Note Appendix B exercises.

2 Quoted in Reuben Job and Norman Shawchuck, *A Guide to Prayers for Ministers and Other Servants* (Nashville: The Upper Room, 1992), p. 60.

Chapter 7

1 Gareth Weldon Icenogle, *Biblical, Theological, and Integrative Foundations for Small Group Ministry* (Pasadena, CA: Fuller Theological Seminary, 1990). I have quoted from his dissertation, adapted from pp. 109-118. His concepts are now published as *Biblical Foundations for Small Group Ministry* (Downers Grove, IL: InterVarsity Press, 1994).

2 *Ibid.*, p. 110.

Chapter 9

1 From an interview with Charles M. Olsen, November 1994.

BIBLIOGRAPHY

Leith Anderson, *A Church for the 21st Century*. Minneapolis, MN: Bethany House Publishers, 1992.

_____, *Dying for Change*. Minneapolis, MN: Bethany House Publishers, 1990.

Jeffrey Arnold, *The Big Book on Small Groups*. Downers Grove, IL: InterVarsity Press, 1992.

George Barna, *What Americans Believe*. Ventura, CA: Regal Books, 1991.

Robert N. Bellah, et al., *Habits of the Heart*. Berkeley, CA: University of California Press, 1985.

Hendrikus Berkhof, *The Doctrine of the Holy Spirit*. Atlanta: John Knox Press, 1976.

Allan Bloom, *The Closing of the American Mind*. New York: Simon and Schuster, 1987.

Dietrich Bonhoeffer, *Life Together*. New York: Harper and Row, 1954.

David J. Bosch, *Transforming Mission*. Maryknoll, NY: Orbis Books, 1991.

Kennon L. Callahan, *Effective Church Leadership*. San Francisco: Harper & Row, 1990.

William Easum, *Dancing with Dinosaurs*. Nashville: Abingdon Press, 1993.

Jacques Ellul, *The New Demons*. New York: The Seabury Press, 1975.

Carl F. George, *Prepare Your Church for the Future*. Tarrytown, NY: Fleming H. Revell Company, 1991.

Denham Grierson, *Transforming a People of God*. Melbourne, Australia: The Joint Board of Christian Education of Australia and New Zealand, 1984.

Stanley Hauerwas and William H. Willimon, *Resident Aliens*. Nashville: Abingdon Press, 1989.

Martin Hengel, *Property and Riches in the Early Church*. Philadelphia: Fortress Press, 1974.

Roberta Hestenes, *Using the Bible in Groups*. Philadelphia: The Westminster Press, 1983.

George G. Hunter III, *How to Reach Secular People*. Nashville: Abingdon Press, 1992.

Gareth Weldon Icenogle, *Biblical Foundations for Small Group Ministry*. Downers Grove, IL: InterVarsity Press, 1994.

Reuben Job and Norman Shawchuck, *A Guide to Prayers for Ministers and Other Servants*. Nashville: The Upper Room, 1992.

Ben Johnson, *95 Theses for the Church*. Decatur, GA: CTS Press, 1995.

_____, *An Adventure in Prayer*. Decatur, GA: CTS Press, 1983.

_____, *Invitation to Pray*. Decatur, GA: CTS Press, 1992.

_____, *To Will God's Will*. Philadelphia: The Westminster Press, 1987.

Leander E. Keck, *The Church Confident*. Nashville: Abingdon Press, 1993.

Loren B. Mead, *The Once and Future Church*. Washington, D.C.: The Alban Institute, 1991.

_____, *Transforming Congregations for the Future*. Washington, D.C.: The Alban Institute, 1994.

Richard Meyer, *One Anothering*. San Diego, CA: LuraMedia, 1990.

Jurgen Moltmann, *The Church in the Power of the Spirit*. New York: Harper & Row, 1975.

Linus J. Morris, *The High Impact Church*. Houston, TX: TOUCH Publications, Inc., 1993.

Lesslie Newbigin, *The Gospel in a Pluralist Society*. Grand Rapids, MI: William B. Eerdmans Publishing Company, 1989.

Ron Nicholas, et al., *Good Things Come in Small Groups*. Downers Grove, IL: InterVarsity Press, 1985.

Charles M. Olsen, *Cultivating Religious Growth Groups*. Philadelphia: The Westminster Press, 1984.

_____, *Transforming Church Boards into Communities of Spiritual Leaders*. Washington, D.C.: The Alban Institute, 1995.

E. Stanley Ott, *Small Group Life*. Decatur, GA: CTS Press, 1994.

_____, *The Vibrant Church*. Ventura, CA: Regal Books, 1989.

_____, *Vision for a Vital Church*. Decatur, GA: CTS Press, 1994.

Eugene Peterson, *The Contemplative Pastor*. Dallas: Word, 1989.

_____, *Earth and Altar*. Downers Grove, IL: InterVarsity Press, 1985.

David Prior, *Creating Community*. Colorado Springs, CO: NavPress, 1992.

Robert H. Ramey, Jr., *Growing Church Leaders*. Decatur, GA: CTS Press, 1995.

Wade Clark Roof, *A Generation of Seekers*. San Francisco: HarperCollins, 1993.

Wade Clark Roof and William McKinney, *American Mainline Religion*. New Brunswick: Rutgers University Press, 1987.

Tex Sample, *U.S. Lifestyles and Mainline Churches*. Louisville: John Knox Press, 1990.

Dorothy Sayers, *Creed or Chaos?* New York: Harcourt Brace, 1949.

Lyle E. Schaller, *It's a Different World!* Nashville: Abingdon Press, 1987.

Samuel Shoemaker, *The Conversion of the Church*. New York: Fleming H. Revell, 1932.

Lee Strobel, *Inside the Mind of Unchurched Harry & Mary*. Grand Rapids, MI: Zondervan Publishing House, 1993.

Marlene Wilson, *How to Mobilize Church Volunteers*. Minneapolis, MN: Augsburg Publishing House, 1983.